T0214234

Lecture Notes in Computer Science 12752

More information about this subseries at http://www.springer.com/series/7408

Raghunath Nambiar · Meikel Poess (Eds.)

Performance Evaluation and Benchmarking

12th TPC Technology Conference, TPCTC 2020
Tokyo, Japan, August 31, 2020
Revised Selected Papers

 Springer

Editors
Raghunath Nambiar
Advanced Micro Devices
Santa Clara, CA, USA

Meikel Poess
Oracle Corporation
Redwood City, CA, USA

ISSN 0302-9743   ISSN 1611-3349 (electronic)
Lecture Notes in Computer Science
ISBN 978-3-030-84923-8   ISBN 978-3-030-84924-5 (eBook)
https://doi.org/10.1007/978-3-030-84924-5

LNCS Sublibrary: SL2 – Programming and Software Engineering

This Springer imprint is published by the registered company Springer Nature Switzerland AG
The registered company address is: Gewerbestrasse 11, 6330 Cham, Switzerland

Preface

The Transaction Processing Performance Council (TPC) is a non-profit organization established in August 1988. Over the years, the TPC has had a significant impact on the computing industry's use of industry-standard benchmarks. Vendors use TPC benchmarks to illustrate performance competitiveness for their existing products, and to improve and monitor the performance of their products under development. Many buyers use TPC benchmark results as points of comparison when purchasing new computing systems.

The information technology landscape is evolving at a rapid pace, challenging industry experts and researchers to develop innovative techniques for evaluation, measurement, and characterization of complex systems. The TPC remains committed to developing new benchmark standards to keep pace with these rapid changes in technology. One vehicle for achieving this objective is the TPC's sponsorship of the Technology Conference Series on Performance Evaluation and Benchmarking (TPCTC) established in 2009. With this conference series, the TPC encourages researchers and industry experts to present and debate novel ideas and methodologies in performance evaluation, measurement, and characterization.

This book contains the proceedings of the 12th TPC Technology Conference on Performance Evaluation and Benchmarking (TPCTC 2020), held in conjunction with the 44th International Conference on Very Large Data Bases (VLDB 2020) in Tokyo, Japan, from August 31 to September 4, 2020.

The hard work and close cooperation of a number of people have contributed to the success of this conference. We would like to thank the members of the TPC and the organizers of VLDB 2020 for their sponsorship; the members of the Program Committee and Publicity Committee for their support; and the authors and the participants who are the primary reason for the success of this conference.

Raghunath Nambiar
Meikel Poess

TPCTC 2020 Organization

General Chairs

Raghunath Nambiar   AMD, USA
Meikel Poess   Oracle, USA

Program Committee

Dippy Aggarwal   Intel, USA
Daniel Bowers   Gartner, USA
Michael Brey   Oracle, USA
Ajay Dholakia   Lenovo, USA
Dhabaleswar Panda   Ohio State University, USA
Tilmann Rabl   TU Berlin, Germany
Reza Taheri   VMware, USA

Publicity Committee

Meikel Poess   Oracle, USA
Andrew Bond   Red Hat, USA
Paul Cao   HPE, USA
Gary Little   Nutanix, USA
Raghunath Nambiar   AMD, USA
Reza Taheri   VMware, USA
Michael Majdalany   L&M Management Group, USA
Forrest Carman   Owen Media, USA
Andreas Hotea   Hotea Solutions, USA

About the TPC

Introduction to the TPC

The Transaction Processing Performance Council (TPC) is a non-profit organization focused on developing industry standards for data centric workloads and disseminating vendor-neutral performance data to the industry. Additional information is available at http://www.tpc.org/.

TPC Memberships

Full Members

Full Members of the TPC participate in all aspects of the TPC's work, including development of benchmark standards and setting strategic direction. The Full Member application can be found at http://www.tpc.org/information/about/app-member.asp.

Associate Members

Certain organizations may join the TPC as Associate Members. Associate Members may attend TPC meetings but are not eligible to vote or hold office. Associate membership is available to non-profit organizations, educational institutions, market researchers, publishers, consultants, governments, and businesses that do not create, market, or sell computer products or services. The Associate Member application can be found at http://www.tpc.org/information/about/app-assoc.asp.

Academic and Government Institutions

Academic and government institutions are invited to join the TPC and a special invitation can be found at http://www.tpc.org/information/specialinvitation.asp.

Contact the TPC

TPC
Presidio of San Francisco
Building 572B (surface)
P.O. Box 29920 (mail)
San Francisco, CA 94129-0920
Voice: 415-561-6272
Fax: 415-561-6120
Email: info@tpc.org

How to Order TPC Materials

All of our materials are now posted free of charge on our website. If you have any questions, please feel free to contact our office directly or by email at info@tpc.org.

Benchmark Status Report

The TPC Benchmark Status Report is a digest of the activities of the TPC and its technical subcommittees. Sign-up information can be found at the following URL: http://www.tpc.org/information/about/email.asp.

TPC 2020 Organization

Full Members (as of May 2021)

Actian
Alibaba
AMD
Cisco
Dell EMC
Fujitsu
Hewlett Packard Enterprise
Hitachi
Huawei
IBM
Inspur
Intel
Lenovo
Microsoft
Nutanix
NVIDIA
Oracle
Red Hat
Transwarp
TTA
VMware

Associate Members

Gartner
University of Coimbra, Portugal
China Academy of Information and Communications Technology
IMEC

TPC 2020 Organization

Steering Committee

Michael Brey (Chair), Oracle
Matthew Emmerton, IBM
Jamie Reding, Microsoft
Ken Rule, Intel
Nicholas Wakou, Dell EMC

Public Relations Committee

Paul Cao, HPE
Gary Little, Nutanix
Chris Elford, Intel
Meikel Poess (Chair), Oracle
Reza Taheri, VMware

Technical Advisory Board

Paul Cao, HPE
Matt Emmerton, IBM
Gary Little, Nutanix
Jamie Reding (Chair), Microsoft
Da-Qi Ren, Huawei
Ken Rul, Intel
Nicholas Wakou, Dell EMC

Technical Subcommittees and Chairs

TPC-C: Jamie Reding, Microsoft
TPC-H: Meikel Poess, Oracle
TPC-E: Matthew Emmerton, IBM
TPC-DS: Meikel Poess, Oracle
TPC-VMS: Reza Taheri, VMware
TPC-DI: Meikel Poess, Oracle
TPCx-HS: Tariq Magdon-Ismail, VMware
TPCx-IoT: Meikel Poess, Oracle
TPCx-BB: Chris Elford, Intel
TPCx-V: Reza Taheri, VMware
TPCx-HCI: Reza Taheri, VMware
TPC-Pricing: Jamie Reding, Microsoft
TPC-Energy: Paul Cao, HPE

Working Groups and Chairs

TPC-AI: Hamesh Patel, Intel
TPC-LDBC: Meikel Poess, Oracle
TPC-OSS: Andy Bond, IBM, Reza Taheri, VMware

Contents

Towards Testing ACID Compliance in the LDBC Social Network Benchmark

Jack Waudby[1], Benjamin A. Steer[2], Karim Karimov[3], József Marton[4], Peter Boncz[5], and Gábor Szárnyas[3,6(✉)]

[1] School of Computing, Newcastle University, Newcastle upon Tyne, England
j.waudby2@newcastle.ac.uk
[2] Queen Mary University of London, London, UK
b.a.steer@qmul.ac.uk
[3] Department of Measurement and Information Systems,
Budapest University of Technology and Economics, Budapest, Hungary
[4] Department of Telecommunications and Media Informatics,
Budapest University of Technology and Economics, Budapest, Hungary
[5] CWI, Amsterdam, Netherlands
boncz@cwi.nl
[6] MTA-BME Lendület Cyber-Physical Systems Research Group, Budapest, Hungary
szarnyas@mit.bme.hu

Abstract. Verifying ACID compliance is an essential part of database benchmarking, because the integrity of performance results can be undermined as the performance benefits of operating with weaker safety guarantees (at the potential cost of correctness) are well known. Traditionally, benchmarks have specified a number of tests to validate ACID compliance. However, these tests have been formulated in the context of relational database systems and SQL, whereas our scope of benchmarking are systems for graph data, many of which are non-relational. This paper presents a set of data model-agnostic ACID compliance tests for the LDBC (Linked Data Benchmark Council) Social Network Benchmark suite's Interactive (SNB-I) workload, a transaction processing benchmark for graph databases. We test all ACID properties with a particular emphasis on isolation, covering 10 transaction anomalies in total. We present results from implementing the test suite on 5 database systems.

1 Introduction

Context. Organizations often complement their existing data processing pipelines with systems dedicated to analyzing graphs such as graph databases [7], graph analytical frameworks [6], and graph streaming engines [8]. The category of *graph databases* broadly refers to transactional systems that use the *property graph* data model, where nodes and edges can be annotated with key-value pairs of attributes. Such systems typically use a schema-free data model and provide operators with stronger expressive power than relational algebra, including transitive reachability, shortest path and regular path queries [2].

© Springer Nature Switzerland AG 2021
R. Nambiar and M. Poess (Eds.): TPCTC 2020, LNCS 12752, pp. 1–17, 2021.
https://doi.org/10.1007/978-3-030-84924-5_1

To stimulate competition between graph database vendors and allow fair comparison of their systems, several benchmarks have been proposed to capture realistic workloads, including those of the Linked Data Benchmark Council (LDBC) [3]. In particular, the LDBC's Social Network Benchmark Interactive workload (SNB-I) was designed to target transactional graph databases [10]. To provide protection against violations of correctness arising from the concurrent execution of transactions and system failures, such transactional databases provide *Atomicity, Consistency, Isolation,* and *Durability* (ACID) guarantees.

Problem. Verifying ACID compliance is an important step in the benchmarking process for enabling fair comparison between systems. The performance benefits of operating with weaker safety guarantees are well established [13] but this can come at the cost of application correctness. To enable apples vs. apples performance comparisons between systems it is expected they uphold the ACID properties. Currently, LDBC provides no mechanism for validating ACID compliance within the SNB-I workflow. A simple solution would be to outsource the responsibility of demonstrating ACID compliance to benchmark implementors. However, the safety properties claimed by a system often do not match observable behaviour [14]. To mitigate this problem, benchmarks such as TPC-C [20] include a number of ACID tests to be executed as part of the benchmarking auditing process. However, we found these tests cannot readily be applied to our context, as they assume lock-based concurrency control and an interactive query API that provides clients with explicit control over a transaction's lifecycle. Modern data systems often use optimistic concurrency control mechanisms [17] and offer a restricted query API, such as only executing transactions as stored procedures [19]. Further, tests that trigger and test row-level locking phenomena, for instance, do not readily map on graph database systems. Lastly, we found these tests are limited in the range of isolation anomalies they cover.

Contribution. This paper presents the design of an implementation agnostic ACID compliance test suite for LDBC SNB-I[1]. Our guiding design principle was to be agnostic of system-level implementation details, relying solely on client observations to determine the occurrence of non-transactional behaviour. Thus all systems can be subjected to the same tests and fair comparisons between SNB-I performance results can be drawn. Tests are described in the context of a graph database employing the property graph data model [2]. Reference implementations are given in Cypher [12], the *de facto* standard graph query language. Particular emphasis is given to testing isolation, covering 10 known anomalies including recently discovered anomalies such as *Observed Transaction Vanishes* [4] and *Fractured Reads* [5]. The test suite has been implemented for 5 database systems.[2] A conscious decision was made to keep tests relatively lightweight, as to not add significant overhead to the benchmarking process.

---

[1] We acknowledge verifying ACID-compliance with a finite set of tests is not possible. However, the goal is not an exhaustive quality assurance test of a system's safety properties but rather to demonstrate that ACID guarantees are supported.

[2] Available at https://github.com/ldbc/ldbc_acid.

Structure. The remainder of the paper is structured as follows: Sect. 2 provides an overview of the SNB-I workload. Sections 3 and 4, describe the Atomicity, and Isolation tests, respectively. In Sect. 5 we present results from running our tests on real-world systems. We discuss related work in Sect. 6 and briefly touch on consistency and durability test in Sect. 7 before concluding in Sect. 8.

2   SNB Interactive Workload

The goal behind LDBC's Social Network Benchmark Interactive workload was to motivate the maturing of transactional graph processing systems. SNB-I defines a schema to represent a network of *Person*s who communicate through *Post*s in *Forum*s. SNB-I consists of 14 complex read and 7 short read queries. There are 8 transactional update operations that insert vertices and edges to the graph. Whilst it is expected a system provides ACID transactions, from a transaction processing perspective, there is little contention in SNB-I's transactions. This makes the occurrence of non-transactional behaviour rare and unfortunately makes the already defined update operations unsuitable for testing most of the ACID properties. To address this limitation, this paper presents a test suite of new transactions. These tests are defined on a small core of LDBC SNB schema (extended with properties for versioning) given in Fig. 1.

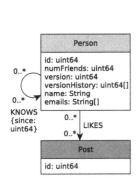

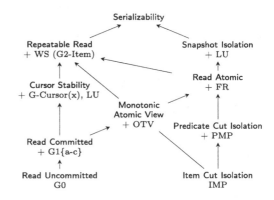

Fig. 1. Graph schema.

Fig. 2. Hierarchy of isolation levels as described in [5]. All anomalies are covered except G-Cursor(x).

3   Atomicity

Atomicity ensures that either all of a transaction's actions are performed, or none are. Two atomicity tests have been developed. **Atomicity-C** checks for every successful commit message a client receives that any data items inserted or modified are subsequently visible. **Atomicity-RB** checks for every aborted transaction that all its modifications are not visible. Tests are executed as follows:

(i) load a graph of **Person** nodes (Listing 1.1) each with a unique **id** and a set of **emails**; (ii) a client executes a full graph scan counting the number of nodes, edges and emails (Listing 1.4) using the result to initialize a counter **committed**; (iii) N transaction instances (Listing 1.2, Listing 1.3) of the required test are then executed, **committed** is incremented for each successful commit; (iii) repeat the full graph scan, storing the result in the variable **finalState**; (iv) perform the anomaly check: **committed=finalState**.

The **Atomicity-C** transaction (Listing 1.2) randomly selects a **Person**, creates a new **Person**, inserts a **KNOWS** edge and appends an **email**. The **Atomicity-RB** transaction (Listing 1.3) randomly selects a **Person**, appends an **email** and attempts to insert a **Person** only if it does not exist. Note, for **Atomicity-RB** if the query API does not offer a **ROLLBACK** statement constraints such as node uniqueness can be utilized to trigger an abort.

```
CREATE (:Person {id: 1, name: 'Alice', emails: ['alice@aol.com']}),
       (:Person {id: 2, name: 'Bob', emails: ['bob@hotmail.com', 'bobby@yahoo.com']})
```

Listing 1.1. Cypher query for creating initial data for the Atomicity transactions.

```
«BEGIN»
MATCH (p1:Person {id: $person1Id})
CREATE (p1)-[k:KNOWS]->(p2:Person)
SET
  p1.emails = p1.emails + [$newEmail],
  p2.id = $person2Id,
  k.creationDate = $creationDate
«COMMIT»
```

```
«BEGIN»
MATCH (p1:Person {id: $person1Id})
SET p1.emails = p1.emails + [$newEmail]
«IF» MATCH (p2:Person {id: $person2Id}) exists
«THEN» «ABORT» «ELSE»
CREATE (p2:Person {id: $person2Id, emails: []})
«END»
«COMMIT»
```

Listing 1.2. Atomicity-C Tx.   **Listing 1.3.** Atomicity-RB Tx.

```
MATCH (p:Person)
RETURN count(p) AS numPersons, count(p.name) AS numNames, sum(size(p.emails)) AS numEmails
```

Listing 1.4. Atomicity-C/Atomicity-RB: counting entities in the graph.

4   Isolation

The gold standard isolation level is Serializability, which offers protection against all possible *anomalies* that can occur from the concurrent execution of transactions. Anomalies are occurrences of non-serializable behaviour. Providing Serializability can be detrimental to performance [13]. Thus systems offer numerous weak isolation levels such as Read Committed and Snapshot Isolation that allow a higher degree of concurrency at the cost of potential non-serializable behaviour. As such, isolation levels are defined in terms of the anomalies they prevent [4,13]. Figure 2 relates isolation levels to the anomalies they proscribe.

SNB-I does not require systems to provide Serializability [3]. However, to allow fair comparison systems must disclose the isolation level used during benchmark execution. The purpose of these isolation tests is to verify that the claimed isolation level matches the expected behaviour. To this end, tests have been developed for each anomaly presented in [5]. Formal definitions for each anomaly are reproduced from [1,5] using their system model which is described below. General design considerations are discussed before each test is described.

4.1 System Model

Transactions consist of an ordered sequence of read and write operations to an arbitrary set of data items, book-ended by a BEGIN operation and a COMMIT or an ABORT operation. In a graph database data items are nodes, edges and properties. The set of items a transaction reads from and writes to is termed its *item read set* and *item write set*. Each write creates a *version* of an item, which is assigned a unique timestamp taken from a totally ordered set (e.g. natural numbers) version i of item x is denoted x_i. All data items have an initial *unborn* version $\bot$ produced by an initial transaction $T_\bot$. The unborn version is located at the start of each item's version order. An execution of transactions on a database is represented by a *history*, H, consisting of (i) each transaction's read and write operations, (ii) data item versions read and written and (iii) commit or abort operations.

There are three types of dependencies between transactions, which capture the ways in which transactions can *directly* conflict. *Read dependencies* capture the scenario where a transaction reads another transaction's write. *Antidependencies* capture the scenario where a transaction overwrites the version another transaction reads. *Write dependencies* capture the scenario where a transaction overwrites the version another transaction writes. Their definitions are as follows:

Read-Depends. Transaction T_j *directly read-depends* (wr) on T_i if T_i writes some version x_k and T_j reads x_k.

Anti-Depends. Transaction T_j *directly anti-depends* (rw) on T_i if T_i reads some version x_k and T_j writes x's next version after x_k in the version order.

Write-Depends. Transaction T_j *directly write-depends* (ww) on T_i if T_i writes some version x_k and T_j writes x's next version after x_k in the version order.

Using these definitions, from a history H a *direct serialization graph DSG(H)* is constructed. Each node in the *DSG* corresponds to a committed transaction and edges correspond to the types of direct conflicts between transactions. Anomalies can then be defined by stating properties about the *DSG*.

The above *item-based* model can be extended to handle *predicate-based* operations [1]. Database operations are frequently performed on set of items provided a certain condition called the *predicate*, P holds. When a transaction executes a read or write based on a predicate P, the database selects a version for each item to which P applies, this is called the version set of the predicate-based denoted as $Vset(P)$. A transaction T_j changes the matches of a predicate-based read $r_i(P_i)$ if T_i overwrites a version in $Vset(P_i)$.

4.2 General Design

Isolation tests begin by loading a *test graph* into the database. Configurable numbers of *write clients* and *read clients* then execute a sequence of transactions on the database for some configurable time period. After execution, results from read clients are collected and an *anomaly check* is performed. In some tests an additional full graph scan is performed after the execution period in order to collect information required for the anomaly check.

The guiding principle behind test design was the preservation of data item's version history – the key ingredient needed in the system model formalization which is often not readily available to clients, if preserved at all. Several anomalies are closely related, tests therefore had to be constructed such that other anomalies could not interfere with or mask the detection of the targeted anomaly. Test descriptions provide (i) informal and formal anomaly definitions, (ii) the required test graph, (iii) description of transaction profiles write and read clients execute, and (iv) reasoning for why the test works.

4.3   Dirty Write

Informally, a *Dirty Write* (Adya's G0 [1]) occurs when updates by conflicting transactions are interleaved. For example, say T_i and T_j both modify items $\{x, y\}$. If version x_i precedes version x_j and y_j precedes version y_i a G0 anomaly has occurred. Preventing G0 is especially important in a graph database in to order to maintain *Reciprocal Consistency* [21].

Definition. A history H exhibits phenomenon G0 if $DSG(H)$ contains a directed cycle consisting entirely of write-dependency edges.

Test. Load a test graph containing pairs of **Person** nodes connected by a **KNOWS** edge. Assign each **Person** a unique **id** and each **Person** and **KNOWS** edge a **versionHistory** property of type list (initially empty). During the execution period, write clients execute a sequence of G0 T_W instances, Listing 1.5. This transaction appends its ID to the **versionHistory** property for each entity in the **Person** pair it matches. Note, transaction IDs are assumed to be globally unique. After execution, a read client issues a G0 T_R for each **Person** pair in the graph, Listing 1.6. Retrieving the **versionHistory** for each entity (2 **Persons** and 1 **KNOWS** edge) in a **Person** pair.

Anomaly Check. For each **Person** pair in the test graph: (i) prune each **versionHistory** list to remove any version numbers that do not appear in all lists; needed to account for interference from *Lost Update* anomalies (Sect. 4.8), (ii) perform an element-wise comparison between **versionHistory** lists for each entity, (iii) if lists do not agree a G0 anomaly has occurred.

Why it Works. Each G0 T_W effectively creates a new version of a **Person** pair. Appending the transaction ID preserves the version history of each entity in the **Person** pair. In a system that prevents G0, each entity of the **Person** pair should experience the *same* updates, in the *same* order. Hence, each position in the **versionHistory** lists should be equivalent. The additional pruning step is needed as *Lost Updates* overwrite a version, effectively erasing it from the history of a data item.

```
MATCH
  (p1:Person {id: $person1Id})
  -[k:KNOWS]->(p2:Person {id: $person2Id})
SET p1.versionHistory = p1.versionHistory + [$tId]
SET p2.versionHistory = p2.versionHistory + [$tId]
SET k.versionHistory  = k.versionHistory  + [$tId]
```

Listing 1.5. Dirty Write (G0) T_W.

```
MATCH (p1:Person {id: $person1Id})
  -[k:KNOWS]->(p2:Person {id: $person2Id})
RETURN
  p1.versionHistory AS p1VersionHistory,
  k.versionHistory  AS kVersionHistory,
  p2.versionHistory AS p2VersionHistory
```

Listing 1.6. Dirty Write (G0) T_R.

4.4   Dirty Reads

Aborted Reads

Informally, an *Aborted Read* (G1a) anomaly occurs when a transaction reads the updates of a transaction that later aborts.

Definition. A history H exhibits phenomenon G1a if H contains an aborted transaction T_i and a committed transaction T_j such that T_j reads a version written by T_i.

Test. Load a test graph containing only **Person** nodes into the database. Assign each **Person** a unique **id** and **version** initialized to 1; any odd number will suffice. During execution, write clients execute a sequence of G1a T_W instances, Listing 1.7. Selecting a random **Person id** to populate each instance. This transaction attempts to set **version=2** (any even number will suffice) but always aborts. Concurrently, read clients execute a sequence of G1a T_R instances, Listing 1.8. This transaction retrieves the **version** property of a **Person**. Read clients store results, which are pooled after execution has finished.

Anomaly Check. Each read should return **version=1** (or any odd number). Otherwise, a G1a anomaly has occurred.

Why it Works. Each transaction that attempts to set **version** to an even number *always* aborts. Therefore, if a transaction reads **version** to be an even number, it must have read the write of an aborted transaction.

```
MATCH (p:Person {id: $personId})
SET p.version = 2
«SLEEP($sleepTime)»
«ABORT»
```

Listing 1.7. Aborted Read (G1a) T_W.

```
MATCH (p:Person {id: $personId})
SET p.version = $even
«SLEEP($sleepTime)»
SET p.version = $odd
```

Listing 1.9. Interm. Read (G1b) T_W.

```
MATCH (p:Person {id: $personId})
RETURN p.version
```

Listing 1.8. Aborted Read (G1a) T_R.

```
MATCH (p:Person {id: $personId})
RETURN p.version
```

Listing 1.10. Interm. Read (G1b) T_R.

Intermediate Reads

Informally, an *Intermediate Read* (Adya's G1b [1]) anomaly occurs when a transaction reads the intermediate modifications of other transactions.

Definition. A history H exhibits phenomenon G1b if H contains a committed transaction T_i that reads a version of an object x_m written by transaction T_j, and T_j also wrote a version x_n such that $m < n$ in x's version order.

Test. Load a test graph containing only **Person** nodes into the database. Assign each **Person** a unique **id** and **version** initialized to 1; any odd number will suffice. During execution, write clients execute a sequence of G1b T_W instances, Listing 1.9. This transaction sets **version** to an even number, then an odd number before committing. Concurrently read-clients execute a sequence of G1b T_R instances, Listing 1.10. Selecting a **Person** by **id** and retrieving its **version** property. Read clients store results which are collected after execution has finished.

Anomaly Check. Each read of **version** should be an odd number. Otherwise, a G1b anomaly has occurred.

Why it Works. The final version installed by an G1b T_W instance is *never* an even number. Therefore, if a transaction reads **version** to be an even number it must have read an intermediate version.

Circular Information Flow

Informally, a *Circular Information Flow* (Adya's G1c [1]) anomaly occurs when two transactions affect each other; i.e. both transactions write information the other reads. For example, transaction T_i reads a write by transaction T_j and transaction T_j reads a write by T_i.

Definition. A history H exhibits phenomenon G1c if $DSG(H)$ contains a directed cycle that consists entirely of read-dependency and write-dependency edges.

Test. Load a test graph containing only **Person** nodes into the database. Assign each **Person** a unique **id** and **version** initialized to 0. Read-write clients are required for this test, executing a sequence of G1c T_{RW}, Listing 1.11. This transaction selects two different **Person** nodes, setting the **version** of one **Person** to the transaction ID and retrieving the **version** from the other. Note, transaction IDs are assumed to be globally unique. Transaction results are stored in format **(txn.id, versionRead)** and collected after execution.

```
MATCH (p1:Person {id: $person1Id}) SET p1.version = $transactionId
MATCH (p2:Person {id: $person2Id}) RETURN p2.version
```

Listing 1.11. G1c T_{RW}.

Anomaly Check. For each result, check the result of the transaction the `versionRead` corresponds to, did not read the transaction of that result. If so a G1c anomaly has occurred.

Why it Works. Consider the result set: $\{(T_1, T_2), (T_2, T_3), (T_3, T_2)\}$. T_1 reads the version written by T_2 and T_2 reads the version written by T_3. Here information flow is unidirectional from T_1 to T_2. However, T_2 reads the version written by T_3 and T_2 reads the version written by T_3. Here information flow is circular from T_2 to T_3 and T_3 to T_2. Thus a G1c anomaly has been detected.

4.5 Cut Anomalies

Item-Many-Preceders

Informally, an *Item-Many-Preceders* (IMP) anomaly [4] occurs if a transaction observes multiple versions of the same item (e.g. transaction T_i reads versions x_1 and x_2). In a graph database this can be multiple reads of a node, edge, property or label. Local transactions (involving a single data item) occur frequently in graph databases, e.g. in *"Retrieve content of a message"* (SNB-I Short Read 4 [3]).

Definition. A history H exhibits IMP if $DSG(H)$ contains a transaction T_i such that T_i directly *item-read-depends* on x by more than one other transaction.

Test. Load a test graph containing **Person** nodes. Assign each **Person** a unique **id** and **version** initialized to 1. During execution write clients execute a sequence of IMP T_W instances, Listing 1.12. Selecting a random **id** and installing a new version of the **Person**. Concurrently read clients execute a sequence of IMP T_R instances, Listing 1.13. Performing multiple reads of the same **Person**; successive reads can be separated by some artificially injected wait time to make conditions more favourable for detecting an anomaly. Both reads within an IMP T_R transaction are returned, stored and collected after execution.

Anomaly Check. Each IMP T_R result set (`firstRead`, `secondRead`) should contain the *same* **Person** version. Otherwise, an IMP anomaly has occurred.

Why it Works. By performing successive reads within the same transaction this test checks that a system ensures consistent reads of the same data item. If the version changes then a concurrent transaction has modified the data item and the reading transaction is not protected from this change.

```
MATCH (p:Person {id: $personId})
SET p.version = p.version + 1
```

Listing 1.12. IMP T_{W}.

```
MATCH (pe:Person {id: $personId}), (po:Post {id: $postId}
CREATE (pe)-[:LIKES]->(po)
```

Listing 1.14. PMP T_{W}.

```
MATCH (p1:Person {id: $personId})
WITH p1.version AS firstRead
«SLEEP($sleepTime)»
MATCH (p2:Person {id: $personId})
RETURN firstRead,
    p2.version AS secondRead
```

Listing 1.13. IMP T_{R}.

```
MATCH (po1:Post {id: $postId})<-[:LIKES]-(pe1:Person)
WITH count(pe1) AS firstRead
«SLEEP($sleepTime)»
MATCH (po2:Post {id: $postId})<-[:LIKES]-(pe2:Person)
RETURN firstRead,
    count(pe2) AS secondRead
```

Listing 1.15. PMP T_{R}.

Predicate-Many-Preceders

Informally, a *Predicate-Many-Preceders* (PMP) anomaly [4] occurs if a transaction observes different versions resulting from the same predicate read (e.g. T_i reads $Vset(P_i) = \{x_1\}$ and $Vset(P_i) = \{x_1, y_2\}$). Pattern matching is a common predicate read operation in a graph database, e.g. query *"Find friends and friends of friends that have been to given countries"* (SNB-I Complex Read 3 [3]).

Definition. A history H exhibits the phenomenon PMP if, for all predicate-based reads $r_i(P_i : Vset(P_i))$ and $r_j(P_j : Vset(P_j))$ in T_k such that the logical ranges of P_i and P_j overlap (call it P_o), the set of transactions that change the matches of P_o for r_i and r_j differ.

Test. Load a test graph containing **Person** and **Post** nodes. Within each node type assign unique **ids**. During execution write clients execute a sequence of PMP T_{W} instances, inserting a **LIKES** edge between a randomly selected **Person** and **Post**, shown in Listing 1.14. Concurrently read clients execute a sequence of PMP T_{R} instances, Listing 1.15. Performing multiple reads of the pattern `(po:Post)<-[:LIKES]-(p:Person)` and counting the number of **LIKES** edges; successive reads can be separated by some artificially injected wait time to make conditions more favourable for detecting an anomaly. Both predicate reads within a PMP T_{R} transaction are returned, stored and collected after test execution.

Anomaly Check. For each PMP T_{R} transaction result set (**firstRead**, **secondRead**), the **firstRead** should be equal to **secondRead**. Otherwise, a PMP anomaly has occurred.

Why it Works. By performing successive predicate reads and counting the number of **LIKES** edges within the same transaction this test checks that a system ensures consistent reads of the same predicate. If the number of **LIKES** edges changes then a concurrent transaction has inserted a new **LIKES** edge and the reading transaction is not protected from this change.

4.6   Observed Transaction Vanishes

Informally, an *Observed Transaction Vanishes* (OTV) anomaly [4] occurs when a transaction observes part of another transaction's updates but not all of them (e.g. T_1 writes x_1 and y_1 and T_2 reads x_1 and $y_\perp$). Before formally defining OTV the *Unfolded Serialization Graph (USG)* must be introduced [1]. The *USG* is specified for an individual transaction, T_i and a history, H and is denoted by $USG(H, T_i)$. In a *USG* the T_i node is split into multiple nodes, one for each action read $r_i(\cdot)$ or write $w_i(\cdot)$ within the transaction. The dependency edges are now incident on the relevant event of T_i. Additionally, actions within T_i are connected by an *order edge* e.g. if T_i reads object y_j then immediately writes on object x an order edge exists from $w_i(x_i)$ to $r_i(y_j)$.

Definition. A history H exhibits phenomenon OTV if $USG(H, T_i)$ contains a directed cycle consisting of (i) exactly one read dependency edge induced by data item x from T_j to T_i and (ii) a set of edges induced by data item y containing at least one anti dependency edge from T_i to T_j. Additionally, T_i's read from y precedes its read from x.

Test. Load a test graph containing a set of cycles of length 4 of **Persons** with same **name** connected by **Knows** edges. Assign each **Person** an **id**, **name** and **version** property (initialized to 1). Note, **id** must be unique across nodes and **name** must be unique across cycles. During execution write clients select a **name**, **id** and executes a sequence of OTV T_W instances, Listing 1.16. This transaction effectively creates a new version of a given cycle. Concurrently read-clients execute a sequence of OTV T_R instances, Listing 1.17. Matching a given cycle and performing multiple reads. Both reads within an OTV T_R are returned, stored and collected after execution.

Anomaly Check. For each OTV T_R result set (**firstRead**, **secondRead**), the maximum **version** in the **firstRead** should be less than or equal to the minimum **version** in the **secondRead**. Otherwise, an OTV anomaly has occurred.

Why it Works. OTV T_W installs a new version of a cycle by updating the **version** property of each **Person**. Therefore when matching a cycle once a transaction has observed some **version** it should *at least* observe this version for every remaining entity in the cycle. Unfortunately, this cannot be deduced from a single read of the cycle as results from matching cycles often does not preserve the order in which graph entities were read. This is solved by making multiple reads of the cycle. The maximum **version** of the **firstRead** determines the minimum **version** of **secondRead**. If this condition is violated then a transaction has observed the effects of a transaction in the **firstRead** then subsequently failed to observe it in the **secondRead** – the observed transaction has vanished!

```
MATCH path =
  (n:Person {id: $personId})
  -[:KNOWS*..4]->(n)
UNWIND nodes(path)[0..4] AS p
SET p.version = p.version + 1
```

```
MATCH p1=(n1:Person {id: $personId})-[:KNOWS*..4]->(n1)
RETURN extract(p IN nodes(p1) | p.version) AS firstRead
«SLEEP($sleepTime)»
MATCH p2=(n2:Person {id: $personId})-[:KNOWS*..4]->(n2)
RETURN extract(p IN nodes(p2) | p.version) AS secondRead
```

Listing 1.16. OTV/FR T_W.   **Listing 1.17.** OTV/FR T_R.

4.7   Fractured Read

Informally, a *Fractured Read* (FR) anomaly [5] occurs when a transaction reads *across* transaction boundaries. For example, if T_1 writes x_1 and y_1 and T_3 writes x_3. If T_2 reads x_1 and y_1, then repeats its read of x and reads x_3 a fractured read has occurred.

Definition. A transaction T_j exhibits phenomenon FR if transaction T_i writes versions x_a and y_b (in any order, where x and y may or may not be distinct items), T_j reads version x_a and version y_c, and $c < b$.

Test. Same as the OTV test.

Anomaly Check. For each FR T_R (Listing 1.17) result set (firstRead, secondRead), all versions across both version sets should be equal. Otherwise, an FR anomaly has occurred.

Why it Works. FR T_W installs a new version of a cycle by updating the version properties on each Person. When FR T_R observes a version every subsequent read in that cycle should read the *same* version as FR T_W (Listing 1.16) installs the same version for all Person nodes in the cycle. Thus, if it observes a different version it has observed the effect of a different transaction and has read across transaction boundaries.

4.8   Lost Update

Informally, a *Lost Update* (LU) anomaly [5] occurs when two transactions concurrently attempt to make conditional modifications to the same data item(s).

Definition. A history H exhibits phenomenon LU if $DSG(H)$ contains a directed cycle having one or more antidependency edges and all edges are induced by the same data item x.

Test. Load a test graph containing Person nodes. Assign each Person a unique id and a property numFriends (initialized to 0). During execution write clients execute a sequence of LU T_W instances, Listing 1.18. Choosing a random Person and incrementing its numFriends property. Clients store local counters (expNumFriends) for each Person, which is incremented each time a Person is selected *and* the LU T_W instance successfully commits. After the execution period the numFriends is retrieved for each Person using LU T_R in Listing 1.19 and expNumFriends are pooled from write clients for each Person.

Anomaly Check. For each Person its numFriends property should be equal to the (global) expNumFriends for that Person.

Why it Works. Clients know how many successful LU T_W instances were issued for a given Person. The observable numFriends should reflect this ground truth, otherwise, an LU anomaly must have occurred.

```
MATCH (p:Person {id: $personId})
SET p.numFriends = p.numFriends + 1
```

Listing 1.18. Lost Update T_W.

```
MATCH (p:Person {id: $personId})
RETURN p.numFriends AS numFriends
```

Listing 1.19. Lost Update T_R.

4.9 Write Skew

Informally, *Write Skew* (WS) occurs when two transactions simultaneously attempted to make *disjoint* conditional modifications to the same data item(s). It is referred to as G2-Item in [1,11].

Definition. A history H exhibits WS if $DSG(H)$ contains a directed cycle having one or more antidependency edges.

Test. Load a test graph containing n pairs of **Person** nodes (p1, p2) for $k = 0, \ldots, n-1$, where the kth pair gets ids p1.id = 2*k+1 and p2.id = 2*k+2, and values p1.value = 70 and p2.value = 80. There is a constraint: p1.value + p2.value > 0. During execution write clients execute a sequence of WS T_W instances, Listing 1.20. Selecting a random **Person** pair and decrementing the value property of one **Person** provided doing so would not violate the constraint. After execution the database is scanned using WS T_R, Listing 1.21.

Anomaly Check. For each **Person** pair the constraint should hold true, otherwise, a WS anomaly has occurred.

Why it Works. Under no Serializable execution of WS T_W instances would the constraint p1.value + p2.value > 0 be violated. Therefore, if WS T_R returns a violation of this constraint it is clear a WS anomaly has occurred.

```
MATCH (p1:Person {id: $person1Id}),
      (p2:Person {id: $person2Id})
«IF (p1.value+p2.value < 100)» «THEN» «ABORT» «END»
«SLEEP($sleepTime)»
pId = «pick randomly between personId1, personId2»
MATCH (p:Person {id: $pId})
SET p.value = p.value - 100
«COMMIT»
```

Listing 1.20. WS T_W.

```
MATCH (p1:Person),
      (p2:Person {id: p1.id+1})
WHERE p1.value + p2.value <= 0
RETURN
  p1.id AS p1id,
  p1.value AS p1value,
  p2.id AS p2id,
  p2.value AS p2value
```

Listing 1.21. WS T_R.

5 Results

Experiment Setup. The ACID-compliance test suite was implemented in a Java application as JUnit tests with all experiments executed on Ubuntu 18.04 running AdoptOpenJDK 11.0.4.hs. All tests were conducted on 4 graph database systems and 1 relational database, consisting of: Neo4j 3.5.20 and 4.1.1, Memgraph 1.0, Dgraph 20.03.3, JanusGraph 0.5.2 (BerkeleyDB 7.5.11 and Cassandra 3.11.0 backends) and PostgreSQL 9.6. For all systems, we used their declarative query languages and the officially recommended Java drivers. For Neo4j 3.5 and Memgraph, queries were defined in Cypher and the `neo4j-java-driver` package version 1.7.0 was used. For Neo4j 4.0, we used the same queries and v4.0.1 of the driver. For the rest of the systems: `dgraph4j` driver v20.03.0 with `GraphQL+-` queries, `janusgraph-driver` v0.5.2 with Gremlin queries, and the `postgresql` driver v42.2.14 with SQL queries, were used respectively.

Analysis. The results for all tests are shown in Table 1. As can be seen here, many of the systems under test met and appeared to exceed their claimed isolation levels. Neo4j promises Read Committed but in fact seems to provide the stronger isolation level Monotonic Atomic View due to proscribing OTV [4]. Interestingly, however, Neo4j 4.0 fails the LU test, which could not be triggered in Neo4j 3.5 even though the two versions claim the same isolation level.[3] We suspect that LU could be triggered in Neo4j 3.5 with a more comprehensive test suite.

Memgraph promises Snapshot Isolation and is successful in this regard, only failing the WS test. Similarly, Dgraph passed all tests without issue, even though it only claims Snapshot Isolation. JanusGraph with the Cassandra backend, whilst offers no isolation due to the lack of arbitrary multi-object transactions, passed a number of tests where this should have caused an issue. Unfortunately, upon investigation, this appears to be due to very stale reads. In a similar vein, the BerkeleyDB implementation was successful across its varying isolation levels, however, exhibited heavy lock contention with as much as 95% of the transactions aborting. PostgreSQL was successful for all of the specified isolation levels,

Table 1. Atomicity (Atomicity-C, Atomicity-RB) and Isolation Tests, ↯ indicates anomaly occurred and ⊗ indicates it did not occur. Notation – *JG:* JanusGraph. ⊛: G1b only passes due to JanusGraph's reads being very stale. ⊖: JanusGraph passed this test, but done so by aborting >95% of transactions. ⊘: PostgreSQL passed this test but with 60% aborts. ◎: Execution timed out after 5 min.

Database	C	RB	Isolation level	G0	G1a	G1b	G1c	OTV	FR	IMP	PMP	LU	WS
Neo4j 3.5	⊗	⊗	Read Committed	⊗	⊗	⊗	⊗	⊗	↯	↯	↯	⊗	↯
Neo4j 4.1	⊗	⊗	Read Committed	⊗	⊗	⊗	⊗	⊗	↯	↯	↯	↯	↯
Memgraph	⊗	⊗	Snapshot Isolation	⊗	⊗	⊗	⊗	⊗	⊗	⊗	⊗	⊗	↯
Dgraph	⊗	⊗	Snapshot Isolation	⊗	⊗	⊗	⊗	⊗	⊗	⊗	⊗	⊗	⊗
JG/BerkeleyDB	⊗	⊗	Read Uncommitted	⊗	⊗	⊛	⊗	↯	↯	⊗	↯	↯	⊖
JG/BerkeleyDB	⊗	⊗	Read Committed	⊖	⊗	⊛	⊖	↯	⊖	⊗	⊖	↯	⊖
JG/BerkeleyDB	⊗	⊗	Repeatable Read	⊖	⊗	⊛	⊖	⊖	⊖	⊗	⊖	⊖	⊖
JG/BerkeleyDB	⊗	⊗	Serializable	⊖	⊗	⊛	⊖	⊖	⊖	⊗	⊖	⊖	⊖
JG/Cassandra	⊗	⊗	Read Uncommitted	⊗	⊗	⊛	⊗	↯	↯	⊛	↯	↯	↯
PostgreSQL	⊗	⊗	Read Committed	⊗	⊗	⊗	⊗	⊗	⊗	⊗	↯	⊗	⊗
PostgreSQL	⊗	⊗	Repeatable Read	⊗	⊗	⊗	⊗	⊗	⊗	⊗	⊗	⊘	⊗
PostgreSQL	⊗	⊗	Serializable	⊗	⊗	⊗	⊗	⊗	⊗	⊗	⊗	◎	⊗

---

[3] Neo4j can guarantee Serializable isolation to avoid these anomalies, however, this requires explicit locks.

however, had notable issues with the LU tests, aborting 60% of transactions at Repeatable Read and timing out with Serializable isolation.

6   Related Work

The challenge of verifying ACID-compliance has been addressed before by transactional benchmarks. For example, TPC-C [20] provides a suite of ACID tests. However, the isolation tests are reliant on lock-based concurrency control, hence are not generalizable across systems. Also, the transactional anomaly test coverage is limited to only four anomalies. The authors of [9] augment the popular YCSB framework for benchmarking transactional NewSQL systems, including a *validation phase* that detects and quantifies consistency anomalies. They permit the definition of arbitrary integrity constraints, checking they hold before and after a benchmark run. Such an approach is not possible within SNB-I due to the restrictive nature of transactional updates and the distinct lack of application-level constraints.

The Hermitage project [16] with the goal of improving understanding of weak isolation, developed a range of hand-crafted isolation tests. This test suite has much higher anomaly coverage but suffers from a problem similar to TPC-C. Test execution is performed by hand, opening multiple terminals to step through the tests.[4] The Jepsen project [14] is not a benchmark rather it addresses correctness testing, traditionally focusing on distributed systems under various failure modes. Most of Jepsen's transactional tests adopt a similar approach to us, executing a suite of transactions with hand-proven invariants. However recently, the project has spawned Elle [15] a black-box transactional anomaly checker. Elle does not rely on hand-crafted tests and can detect every anomaly in [1] (except for predicate-based anomalies) from an arbitrary transaction history.

7   Consistency and Durability Tests

While this paper mainly focused on *atomicity* and *isolation* from the ACID properties, we provide a short overview of the other two aspects. *Durability* tests are already part of the benchmark specification [3], while adding complex *consistency* checks is left for future work.

Durability is a hard requirement for SNB-I and checking it is part of the auditing process. The durability test requires the execution of the SNB-I workload and uses the LDBC workload driver. Note, the database and the driver must be configured in the same way as would be used in the performance run. First, the database is subject to a warm-up period. Then after 2 h of simulation execution, the database processes will be terminated, possibly by disconnecting the entire machine or by a hard process kill. Note that turning the machine off

---

[4] We initially experimented with Hermitage but found it difficult to induce anomalies that relied on fast timings due to some graph databases offering limited client-side control over transactions, with all statements submitted in one batch.

may not be possible in cloud tests. The database system is then restarted and each client issues a read for the value of the last entity (node or edge) it received a successful commit message for, that should produce a correct response.

Consistency is defined in terms of constraints: the database remains consistent under updates; i.e. no constraint is violated. Relational database systems usually support primary- and foreign-key constraints, as well as domain constraints on column values and sometimes also support simple within-row constraints. Graph database systems have a diversity of interfaces and generally do not support constraints, beyond sometimes domain and primary key constraints (in case indexes are supported). As such, we leave them out of scope for LDBC SNB. However, we do note that we anticipate that graph database systems will evolve to support constraints in the future. Beyond equivalents of the relational ones, property graph systems might introduce graph-specific constraints, such as (partial) compliance to a schema formulated on top of property graphs, rules that guide the presence of labels or structural graph constraints such as connectedness of the graph, absence of cycles, or arbitrary well-formedness constraints [18].

8   Conclusion and Future Work

In this paper, we discussed the challenges of testing ACID properties on graph databases systems and compiled a test suite of 2 atomicity and 10 isolation tests. We have implemented the proposed tests on 5 database systems, consisting of 3400 lines of code in total.Our findings show that Neo4j, Memgraph, and Dgraph satisfy their claimed isolation levels, and, in some cases, they even seem to provide stronger guarantees. We found that JanusGraph is unfit to be used in transactional workloads. PostgreSQL satisfies the selected isolation levels but in the LU tests this came at a cost of aborting the majority of the transactions (Repeatable Read) or causing a timeout (Serializable).

Looking ahead, in the short term, we will include these tests in the LDBC SNB specification [3] and use them for auditing the ACID-compliance of SUTs. In the long term, we plan to extend the tests to incorporate complex consistency constraints and add tests specifically designed for distributed databases [21].

Acknowledgements. J. Waudby was supported by the Engineering and Physical Sciences Research Council, Centre for Doctoral Training in Cloud Computing for Big Data [grant number EP/L015358/1]. B. Steer was supported by the Engineering and Physical Sciences Research Council and Alan Turing Institute [grant number EP/T001569/1]. P. Boncz was partially supported by the SQIREL-GRAPHS NWO project. G. Szárnyas was partially supported by the MTA-BME Lendület Cyber-Physical Systems Research Group.

References

1. Adya, A.: Weak consistency: a generalized theory and optimistic implementations for distributed transactions. Ph.D. dissertation, MIT (1999)

2. Angles, R., et al.: Foundations of modern query languages for graph databases. ACM Comput. Surv. **50**(5), 68:1–68:40 (2017)
3. Angles, R., et al.: The LDBC Social Network Benchmark. CoRR, abs/2001.02299 (2020)
4. Bailis, P., et al.: Highly available transactions: virtues and limitations. VLDB **7**, 181–192 (2013)
5. Bailis, P., Fekete, A., Ghodsi, A., Hellerstein, J.M., Stoica, I.: Scalable atomic visibility with RAMP transactions. ACM Trans. Database Syst. **41**, 1–45 (2016)
6. Batarfi, O., et al.: Large scale graph processing systems: survey and an experimental evaluation. Cluster Comput. **18**(3), 1189–1213 (2015)
7. Besta, M., et al.: Demystifying graph databases: analysis and taxonomy of data organization, system designs, and graph queries. CoRR, abs/1910.09017 (2019)
8. Besta, M., et al.: Practice of streaming and dynamic graphs: concepts, models, systems, and parallelism. CoRR, abs/1912.12740 (2019)
9. Dey, A., Fekete, A., Nambiar, R., Röhm, U.: YCSB+T: benchmarking web-scale transactional databases. In: ICDE, pp. 223–230. IEEE Computer Society (2014)
10. Erling, O., et al.: The LDBC social network benchmark: interactive workload. In: SIGMOD, pp. 619–630. ACM (2015)
11. Fekete, A., Liarokapis, D., O'Neil, E.J., O'Neil, P.E., Shasha, D.E.: Making snapshot isolation serializable. ACM Trans. Database Syst. **30**(2), 492–528 (2005)
12. Francis, N., et al.: Cypher: an evolving query language for property graphs. In: SIGMOD, pp. 1433–1445. ACM (2018)
13. Gray, J., Lorie, R.A., Putzolu, G.R., Traiger, I.L.: Granularity of locks and degrees of consistency in a shared data base. pp. 365–394 (1976)
14. Kingsbury, K.: Jepsen analyses (2020). http://jepsen.io/analyses
15. Kingsbury, K., Alvaro, P.: Elle: Inferring isolation anomalies from experimental observations. CoRR, abs/2003.10554 (2020)
16. Kleppmann, M.: Hermitage: testing transaction isolation levels (2020). https://github.com/ept/hermitage
17. Pavlo, A., Aslett, M.: What's really new with NewSQL? SIGMOD Rec. **45**, 45–55 (2016)
18. Semeráth, O., et al.: Formal validation of domain-specific languages with derived features and well-formedness constraints. Softw. Syst. Model. **16**(2), 357–392 (2017)
19. Stonebraker, M., et al.: The end of an architectural era (it's time for a complete rewrite). In: VLDB, pp. 1150–1160. ACM (2007)
20. TPC. TPC Benchmark C, revision 5.11. Technical report (2010). http://www.tpc.org/tpc_documents_current_versions/pdf/tpc-c_v5.11.0.pdf
21. Waudby, J., Ezhilchelvan, P., Webber, J., Mitrani, I.: Preserving reciprocal consistency in distributed graph databases. In: PaPoC at EuroSys. ACM (2020)

EXPOSE: Experimental Performance Evaluation of Stream Processing Engines Made Easy

Espen Volnes[(✉)], Thomas Plagemann, Vera Goebel, and Stein Kristiansen

Department of Informatics, University of Oslo, Oslo, Norway
{espenvol,plageman,goebel,steikr}@ifi.uio.no

Abstract. Experimental performance evaluation of stream processing engines (SPE) can be a great challenge. Aiming to make fair comparisons of different SPEs raises this bar even higher. One important reason for this challenge is the fact that these systems often use concepts that require expert knowledge for each SPE. To address this issue, we present Expose, a distributed performance evaluation framework for SPEs that enables a user through a declarative approach to specify experiments and conduct them on multiple SPEs in a fair way and with low effort. Experimenters with few technical skills can define and execute distributed experiments that can easily be replicated. We demonstrate Expose by defining a set of experiments based on the existing NEXMark benchmark and conduct a performance evaluation of Flink, Beam with the Flink runner, Siddhi, T-Rex, and Esper, on powerful and resource-constrained hardware.

Keywords: Performance evaluation · Stream processing · Distributed experiments

1 Introduction

Distributed Stream Processing Engines (SPE) process tuples at potentially high rates, perform filter operations, aggregation operations, and derive higher-level events. These are performed without the need to store the tuples persistently. Such systems are becoming more and more relevant for an increasing number of applications, ranging from classical financial services to sensor-based smart-* systems. As such, stream processing becomes highly relevant for fog networks where Big Data processing shifts from only occurring at resourceful data centers to access points closer to data sources. That means data is processed on resource-constrained systems close to the client and in resourceful data centers. This diversity in terms of applications and processing environments implies that the age of "one size fits all" has ended for SPEs [23]; and naturally leads to a large number of different SPEs, all with their particular strength and weaknesses. These include SPEs aimed towards data centers for high concurrency, throughput, and integration possibilities, like Apache Flink, Esper Enterprise Edition,

© Springer Nature Switzerland AG 2021
R. Nambiar and M. Poess (Eds.): TPCTC 2020, LNCS 12752, pp. 18–34, 2021.
https://doi.org/10.1007/978-3-030-84924-5_2

and Apache Storm, as well as SPEs suitable for relatively resource-constrained systems, like the library versions of Siddhi and Esper. Furthermore, there are different types of SPEs, including Data Stream Management Systems, Complex Event Processing (CEP) systems, and Big Data processing systems.

With many SPEs available, each with its own qualities, choosing the correct one for a given application is a challenge. Benchmarks might help, but there are limitations in the existing SPE benchmarks, and a given benchmark might not reflect the needs for a particular application and its processing environment. Comparative experimental performance evaluation would be the best foundation, but these require expert knowledge for all involved SPEs to achieve a fair comparison. Furthermore, experiments require a lot of effort, including configuration management, workload generation, and monitoring to gather performance numbers. Experimenting with distributed SPEs is even more complex. To overcome these challenges, we present in this paper a framework to simplify experimental performance evaluation of distributed SPEs, called Expose. Before we describe the fairness aspect in more detail, we briefly identify other use cases for Expose: (1) researchers that develop new SPE (mechanisms) and want to compare them with state-of-the-art solutions, (2) developers that want to identify bottlenecks in SPEs, (3) users that want to understand the impact of different processing environments on the performance of an SPE, and (4) committees that want to define benchmarks.

While heterogeneity in SPEs is an important reason to perform comparative experiments, it is also the main reason why it is difficult to do. Different SPEs use different abstractions, concepts, and lack a definite standard. An expert for one system might not integrate another system as well in an experiment. This can lead to unfairness and bias, and a system might perform best because the developer knows it the best, not because it is best for the application. Ideally, we would like to run experiments by using for all SPEs a common set of concepts like "Deploy queries," "Define data stream," "Add sink for a stream," which are all implemented in the different SPEs.

To the best of our knowledge, no existing work provides such a generic interface for executing complex distributed SPE experiments. Apache Beam and the standardization initiative in [4] aim for a unified interface for SPEs and other data management systems, but lack support for experimental performance evaluation of SPEs. The PEEL experiment framework [5] provides users with the ability to define experiments with less effort than normal, but each SPE still needs to be treated in a different way when defining experiments. Moreover, PEEL does not enable the user to configure the distribution of the SPEs. Multiple microbenchmarks exist that address individual stream processing operators, but they do not test SPEs on application level and lack distribution.

We aim to reduce the workload when defining and executing distributed SPE experiments through a declarative approach. Our proposal is a framework for defining distributed SPE experiments and automating the execution of the experiments. The same experiment definition can be executed with all supported SPEs. A user can utilize any dataset for transmitting tuples and define schemas to be used in experiments. Moreover, the user can choose to trace new metrics and events of interest, which can, for example, be used to create new benchmarks. Stream topologies can be set up in the same way for all supported SPEs, regardless of whether the SPE system internally uses the publish/subscribe or data source and data sink abstractions.

The core of Expose is an API based on a set of SPE tasks. These are used to define the experiments with commands like "Add Query 5 to Node 2," "Wait until the stream has ended on Node 2," and "Send Dataset 2 as a stream on Node 1." To support a new SPE in Expose, we expect experts to implement a "wrapper" for the SPE that supports these commands. This limited one-time effort should allow for fairness since an expert should be able to implement it in the best possible way. Through this declarative approach, non-experts with a basic understanding of SPE concepts are able to define complex distributed experiments, including the performance metrics of interest. The experiments are automatically executed, and the results are prepared for the experimenter. A summary of our contributions is as follows:

- framework for evaluating and comparing distributed SPEs in a fair and replicable way,
- declarative API for the execution of SPEs,
- implementation of the API in five SPE systems (Flink [6], Beam [1], Siddhi [24], Esper [2], and T-Rex [8]),
- open-source repository that contains the code, available at GitHub[1],
- implementation of a well-known SPE benchmark in Expose, and
- execution of the benchmark on the supported SPEs.

The paper is structured as follows. Section 2 presents the framework. In Sect. 3, we demonstrate the use of the framework. Section 4 discusses related works, and Sect. 5 concludes the paper.

2   Design

The main innovation introduced by Expose is the ability to define simple distributed SPE experiments with multiple SPEs. The output of the systems is homogeneous and thus directly comparable. The experimenter does not need to know the internal workings of these systems, but must rather define experiments as a list of tasks to be executed on the specified node in the experiment, each of which represents one SPE instance or cluster in the experiment topology. Examples of tasks are adding a node as next hop for a given stream, deploying SQL queries, and streaming a dataset to the next hops. How these tasks are executed on each specific SPE is up to a "wrapper" that is implemented by an expert in that SPE.

The target user for Expose is anyone with an interest in conducting a performance evaluation of SPEs. Benchmarks are great for performance evaluation, but new ones are always needed because they often have a narrow focus [14]. The downside of benchmarks is that they are rigid and require all stakeholders

---

[1] GitHub repository available at https://github.com/espv/expose.

to agree that the benchmark provides meaningful results [9]. Sometimes, custom benchmarks or performance evaluations are preferable, which requires a way of defining, changing, and executing them. Our goal is to give the user the ability to easily define and execute their own performance evaluation such that they can gain with a low effort the type of results and insights they are interested in. They can select custom datasets, measurements, and parameters to use for the evaluation, and set up the stream topology with an arbitrary number of nodes.

2.1 Experiments

An SPE experiment is a clearly defined execution of SPEs that uses an experiment definition as input and gives performance results as output. The experiment definition includes all information needed to execute the experiment. Therefore, the experiments are repeatable. In order to use different SPEs in the experiments, Expose works in a declarative way. The experimenter decides what tasks should be executed, but not how. We remove the need for the experimenter to understand the specifics of the SPE. To make the experiment definition human-readable, we use the YAML configuration format.

If the output from SPEs is system-independent, analysis of the results and comparison among the systems becomes much more feasible. To achieve this, it is necessary to implement or reuse a minimalistic tracing module for each SPE that can be used to trace arbitrary events in the code. The reason to do this instead of using the SPE's internal runtime logs is to ensure that the output trace is in the same format for every SPE. The SPE expert adds tracepoints, each with its own ID, and then the experimenter can activate or deactivate tracepoints in experiments. Therefore, the experiment definition should specify not only the tasks to be executed, but also what events are traced during the experiment.

The lack of a standardized query language for SPEs is well known and resulted, for example, in the popular Apache Beam and "One SQL" [4] standardization initiative. Apache Beam can imply performance penalties ranging from factor 4 to 58, depending on the SPE and operators being used [11]. This work is focused on performance evaluation that results in reliable performance numbers. As such, it is important that the solution is lightweight with minimal impact on the performance evaluation and support tasks that are necessary to perform experiments and to deliver quite reliable performance numbers. Therefore, we do not build upon Beam, but instead create an independent solution that can evaluate all kinds of SPEs, including unifying systems such as Beam.

For any experiment, the SQL queries, stream schemas, and datasets need to be given in the experiment definition. Each element of the experiment definition is SPE-agnostic except for the SQL queries. Even though the SPEs support an SQL-like language, their syntax may be completely different from each other, and the same features might not be supported in all SPEs. The SPE wrappers can translate small variations in syntax, but translating complex SQL queries without any performance penalty is outside the scope of this paper.

On the other hand, we can define SPE tasks, which are common across all SPEs. Examples are "send dataset as a stream," "add next hop for stream ID," and "deploy SQL query." These tasks are materialized as an API that each SPE wrapper implements. The SPE tasks are defined based on an analysis of the SPEs that we study in this paper. As such, the set of tasks might not be comprehensive, but it is sufficient to describe a wide variety of distributed stream processing experiments. To create an SPE wrapper, the SPE expert maps the tasks to the SPE by using the special functionality offered by the SPE. That way, we preserve the unique capabilities of the SPEs while enabling different SPEs to run the same experiments.

In Table 1, we list all SPE tasks that are needed for the experiments. We distinguish between tasks that are manual and explicitly added to the experiment definition by the experimenter and tasks that are automatically issued by the SPE wrapper. The SPE tasks describe how to set up or expand stream topologies with addNextHop. Stream schemas can be added with addSchemas. SQL queries can be deployed on the specified node with deployQueries and removed with clearQueries. The runtime environment can be started with startRuntimeEnv and stopped with stopRuntimeEnv. The level of parallelism can be set with setParallelism. Streaming datasets to the next hops can be done with sendDsAsStream, realistically using timestamps from the tuples, as fast as possible, or with an arbitrary rate. Tuples from a stream can be written to file using writeStreamToCsv.

In addition to the SPE tasks, experiments require another class of tasks called experiment tasks, listed in Table 2. These tasks are necessary for the execution of experiments, most of which are automatically issued to the SPE nodes by the coordinator. Examples of experiment tasks include looping through a sequence of tasks a given number of times and waiting until no tuple has been received in a number of milliseconds.

Table 1. SPE tasks

SPE tasks	Manual	Description
addNextHop	Yes	Add next hop to a stream
deployQueries	Yes	Deploy specified query a given number of times
startRuntimeEnv	Yes	Start runtime environment
stopRuntimeEnv	Yes	Stop runtime environment
setParallelism	Yes	Set desired level of parallelism for processing tuples
sendDsAsStream	Yes	Convert dataset to stream, and send it to all next hops
clearQueries	Yes	Remove all existing queries
writeStreamToCsv	Yes	Write tuples from stream to file
addSchemas	No	Add stream schemas
startExperiment	No	First task executed by SPEs in the experiment
endExperiment	No	Final task executed by SPEs in the experiment

Distribution is required in most SPE applications, but it makes experimentation more complex. It is not trivial to ensure that the tasks in the experiments

Table 2. Experiment tasks

Experiment task	Manual	Description
traceTuple	Yes	Custom-defined tracepoint
retEndOfStream	Yes	Task that returns from the SPE when no tuples have been received for a specified number of milliseconds
loopTasks	Yes	Coordinator task to loop through a sequence of tasks a given number of iterations
setNidToAddress	No	Coordinator broadcasts mapping from node ID to address when new SPE instance/cluster registers
addTpIds	No	Setup task to let SPEs know which tracepoints should be active
startExperiment	No	First task executed by SPEs in the experiment
endExperiment	No	Final task executed by SPEs in the experiment

are executed in the correct order, at the correct time, and by the correct node. Moreover, we need to decide what entity is responsible for deciding which node executes which task and when. To support distributed experiments and give the experimenter full control of the end-to-end data stream pipeline, we introduce a `coordinator`, as illustrated in Fig. 1. m SPE nodes participate in this experiment, each of which is an instance of an SPE or an SPE cluster. Arbitrarily many SPE nodes can run on a single machine. The coordinator has an overview of these nodes and is the entity that issues tasks to them. The tasks in the experiment definition must denote which node should execute the task. We introduce the node ID to make the experiment definitions fully reusable and avoid specifying IP addresses and port numbers in the experiment definition. During the start phase of an experiment, each SPE node registers with the coordinator and provides their node ID and port on which the other nodes can reach them. The coordinator then broadcasts the mapping from node ID to the IP address and port to the rest of the SPE nodes. This way, all SPE nodes know how to transmit tuples to the next hop, and the coordinator knows to which address to transmit tasks. As such, the end-to-end pipeline can be specified in the experiment definition without low-level details such as IP addresses and port numbers that are dependent on the particular execution environment of an SPE.

The experimenter starts the coordinator and SPE nodes, either manually or through a reusable script. Each SPE node is started with the coordinator's address and uses it to connect to the coordinator's TCP server. Therefore, the SPE nodes can be on the same machine as the coordinator, on a different machine in the same local area network, or anywhere else, as long as the coordinator is accessible. The coordinator and the SPE instances/clusters can, for instance, be started remotely with software such as Ansible [13], in which commands can execute remotely on another server. The experimenter only needs to install the SPEs and provide the Ansible node names in the script. These tasks can be done by someone with limited technical skills.

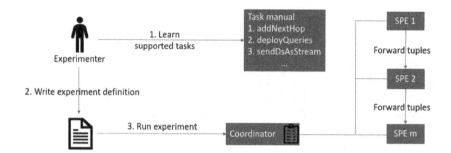

Fig. 1. Workflow of performing an experiment with Expose

2.2   Measurements and Analysis

The overall goal of Expose is to get performance numbers from executing SPE experiments. This section explains how Expose supports the analysis and comparison of results. The analysis is based on the output execution traces from the SPEs. Two types of trace events are captured, listed in Table 3: processing and state events. Processing events are used to calculate throughput and execution time. Examples of these include tracing when a tuple is received and when it is finished processing. With state events, we can calculate the execution time and throughput with respect to, e.g., the number of deployed queries or the size of the windows. Examples of state events include when a query is deployed, when all queries are cleared and when a new data sink or data source is added.

Table 3. Tracepoints

Tracepoint names	Type
Start experiment	State
Receive Tuple	Processing
Finished Processing Tuple	Processing
Deploy Query	State
End of stream	State
Increase number of sources	State
Increase number of sinks	State

The processing and state trace events can be used to visualize and represent the results in various ways. The processing events are used to calculate the performance metric, and the state events are used to calculate the control parameter. In a 2D graph, one would typically see the value of the performance metric on the y-axis and the control parameter on the x-axis.

2.3   SPE Wrapper

In this section, we address three challenges to overcome when attempting to create an SPE wrapper to include in Expose. They are (1) to implement the task API, (2) implementing a communication module between the wrapper and the coordinator, and (3) implementing a tracing module for the wrapper. The task API consists of the methods listed in Tables 1 and 2. The main challenge involves mapping the SPE tasks to the functionality offered by the SPE. For instance, setting the next hop for streams in Esper, Siddhi, and T-Rex involves transmitting the produced tuples to the recipients within a method call, whereas in Beam and Flink, it requires setting up the data pipeline before the runtime environment has started. When tuples are produced, they are automatically transmitted to the next hops. How to deploy SQL queries depends completely on the abstractions and data structures used in the SPE. Sending a dataset as a stream is challenging to implement because most SPEs have their own way of ensuring that the tuples conform to the schemas. Moreover, how tuples are sent to the next-hop nodes depends on which connector is used by the SPE, e.g., TCP or Kafka. When the API is implemented, the SPE wrapper can execute experiments, but only locally.

To enable the SPE to participate in distributed experiments, we need the communication module between the wrapper and the coordinator. At startup, the coordinator waits for SPE nodes to register by contacting its TCP server. The wrapper is provided the address information to the coordinator, and the communication module establishes a connection with the coordinator. This module starts an infinite loop where it waits for tasks to execute from the coordinator. When it receives one, it calls the corresponding method in the wrapper with the provided arguments. After the task is finished executing, it replies to the coordinator with the return value and waits for another task to execute. The communication pattern between the SPE wrappers and the coordinator is the same, regardless of the SPE. Therefore, Expose can execute experiments with different SPEs. This module can also be entirely reused for a new SPE if it is written in the same programming language as a previous SPE.

The final component to implement in an SPE wrapper is the tracing module. This module is required to be able to record and retrieve results from the experiments. The most important requirement for this module is that all the SPEs that participate in the experiment have a similar module that causes minimal overhead to the experiments. As with the communication module, this module can be reused if the SPE is written in the same language as another SPE with a ready wrapper.

We have created SPE wrappers for Siddhi 5.0.0, Esper 8.3.0, T-Rex, Flink 1.9.1, and Beam 2.21.0. Siddhi, Esper, Flink, and Beam are Java-based SPEs, whereas T-Rex is a C++-based SPE. Beam is by itself not an SPE, but a system that gives a unified SPE interface and can be used to execute a variety of SPE engines, such as Flink and several other SPEs. We choose in the experiments later to run it with the Flink runner, which we call Beam Flink, to investigate the performance difference between it and Flink.

3   Use-Case: NEXMark Benchmark

The goal of this section is to demonstrate that (1) Expose can be used to evaluate and compare various SPEs, (2) how easy it is to perform such experiments, and (3) that we can define benchmarks with Expose with low effort. To achieve this, we have on, the one hand, implemented wrappers for Flink, Beam, Esper, Siddhi, and T-Rex, and on the other hand, implemented an experiment definition for a well-known and accepted benchmark called NEXMark [25]. The benchmark describes a set of eight queries that process data from three schemas: Person, Auction, and Bid. We implement all the queries in addition to a passthrough query that only selects and forwards Bid tuples, which comprise 92% of the dataset. Each query is used in one experiment. Below, we describe the queries:

0. Passthrough: forwards all Bid tuples.
1. Currency Conversion: uses a user-defined function to convert the Bid prices from dollar to euro.
2. Selection: filters Bid tuples based on auction ID.
3. Local Item Suggestion: a join between Auction and Person tuples with predicates on the Person.state and Auction.category.
4. Average Price for a Category: the average price of auction categories.
5. Hot Items: the auction with the most Bid tuples is selected.
6. Average Selling Price By Seller: the average price of the auction items of each seller is selected.
7. Highest Bid: the Bid tuple with the highest price is selected.
8. Monitor New Users: Person tuples are joined with Auction tuples that were received within 12 h of each other.

We execute the benchmark on two different servers: a powerful Intel Xeon server with 48 GB RAM and two Intel Xeon Gold 5215 SP CPUs with ten cores, each running at 2.50 GHz, and a weak Raspberry Pi 4 B+ (RPI) with a Broadcom BCM2711 CPU that has four cores running at 1.5 GHz, with 4 GB RAM. The experiment topology consists of three SPE instances: the data driver that produces the tuples, the system under test (SUT) that processes the tuples according to the deployed query, and the sink node that receives all the produced tuples. The data driver and sink run on the same hardware as the coordinator, and the SUT runs on either the Intel Xeon server or the RPI. This way, the SUT is completely isolated and is not affected by Expose or the other SPEs. NEXMark leaves the size of the dataset open, but it provides a dataset generator that enables us to generate datasets of different sizes. We use a dataset with size 1,000,000 tuples for the Intel Xeon server, and the RPI uses 40,000 tuples. In some of the queries, the memory consumption increases for each incoming tuple. Thus, the small amount of RAM available on the RPI makes it impossible for the RPI to process a larger dataset.

The experiment instructions used for all the queries are given in Listing 1.1, where only query_id and output_stream_id differ for each query. Each SPE runs the experiment for all its supported queries and requires no changes to the experiment instructions. The experiment is started by setting up the data stream topology with **addNextHop**, i.e., set Node 2 as a recipient of the streams in the dataset, and Node 3 as the recipient of the output stream from the query. After the topology is set up, a loop with ten iterations starts where the dataset is sent as a stream in each iteration. From the traces, we calculate the throughput of each SPE and query as the average number of tuples per second (TPS) and the relative standard deviation (RSD). Only the final five iterations in the loop are used for these calculations; the first five iterations serve as a warmup to enable any runtime optimizations to activate, which can have a significant effect on performance in Java.

Listing 1.1. NEXmark experiment instructions

```
# Set Node 1 to send Auction, Bid and Person to Node 2
- {task: addNextHop, arguments: [1, 2], node: 1}  # Person stream
- {task: addNextHop, arguments: [2, 2], node: 1}  # Auction stream
- {task: addNextHop, arguments: [3, 2], node: 1}  #  Bid stream
# Set Node 2 to send output stream to Node 3
- {task: addNextHop, arguments: [output_stream_id, 3], node: 2}
# Deploy query to Node 2
- {task: deployQueries, arguments: [query_id, 1], node: 2}
# Stream the dataset ten times
- {task: loopTasks, node: coordinator, arguments: [10, [
  {task: startRuntimeEnv, node: 2},
  {task: startRuntimeEnv, node: 3},
  {task: sendDsAsStream, arguments: [8], node: 1},
  {task: retEndOfStream, node: 3, arguments: [2000]},
  {task: traceTuple, node: 2, arguments: [200, []]},
  {task: stopRuntimeEnv, node: 2},
  {task: stopRuntimeEnv, node: 3}]]}
```

Not all the SPEs support the necessary query processing functionality for these specific queries. Therefore, even though all the SPE wrappers support the same tasks, some SPEs do not run all the queries. For instance, T-Rex is a CEP system that only supports Query 0. Beam does not support joining streams without special window constructs, and so, it does not run Queries 3, 4, 6, and 8. Moreover, Query 6 requires the ability to group output by a key and then limit the number of tuples in each group to ten tuples, which is not supported by the SQL language of any of the SPEs. Therefore, we modify Query 6 to look at all the tuples instead, for all the SPEs. Queries 4–6 define sliding windows over multiple aggregations, which is only supported in Flink. The problem is that performing aggregations over aggregations, such as calculating the average of several maximum values, requires the ability to invalidate outdated tuples. A newly received tuple might replace an old maximum, and so, the old tuple should be removed from the average. As far as we know, only Flink supports this feature among the SPEs. Therefore, Siddhi and Esper perform a variation of the queries using tumbling windows instead of sliding windows, which does not require this feature. A tumbling window version of Query 4–6 for Flink and Beam is not possible either because of their limited support for tumbling windows using an external timestamp and so cannot execute them. Therefore, we have a sliding and tumbling window version of Query 4–6.

Listings 1.2, 1.3, 1.4 and 1.5 show the implementations of Query 4 for Siddhi, Flink and Esper, in addition to the template query. Notice how the implementations are completely different, as the SPEs do not (1) support the same query processing functionality, and (2) use different syntax among each other. In particular, Siddhi implements this query as three separate queries, where the output from the first query is used as input to the second, and the output from the second query is used for the third. Esper implements it as two queries where the output from the first query is used as input to the second, and Flink implements it as a single query with a subquery. Siddhi requires three queries because it must separate the (1) join between Auction and Bid from (2) the maximum aggregation that uses the tumbling window, and (3) the average aggregation. With Esper, we can combine the first two queries and only have to separate the last average aggregation. Flink supports subqueries, and therefore performs the maximum aggregation in the subquery and the average aggregation in the top-level of the query. Beam also supports the syntax of the query that Flink uses, but it has limited support with regard to joining streams, and therefore, we do not execute this query with Beam. T-Rex also has no support for this query. This issue of different SQL languages and query processing features illustrates the challenge with comparing SPEs, and thus, why Expose requires each SPE explicitly to have its version of a given query in the experiment definition.

Listing 1.2. NEXMark Query 4 with sliding window in Siddhi

```
from  Bid#window.time(999 years) as B
join  Auction#window.time(999 years) as A on A.id == B.auction
select  B.dateTime, B.price, A.category, B.auction, A.expires
insert into MQ4_1;

from  MQ4_1#window.externalTimeBatch(dateTime, 1 min)[dateTime < expires]
select  max(price) as final, category group by auction, category
insert into MQ4_2;

from  MQ4_2#window.time(999 years)
select  avg(final) as price, category group by category
insert into OutQuery4;
```

Listing 1.3. NEXMark Query 4 with tumbling window in Flink

```
select  avg(final), category
from  (select MAX(B.price) AS final, A.category from Auction A, Bid B
     where A.id=B.auction and B.dateTime2 < A.expires2
     group by A.id, A.category) Q
group by category
```

Listing 1.4. NEXMark Query 4 with sliding window in Esper

```
insert into MQ4_2
select  max(B.price) as final, A.category as category
from  Auction#time(999 min) A, Bid#ext_timed_batch(dateTime, 1 min) B
where  A.id = B.auction and B.dateTime < A.expires
group by B.auction, A.category;

insert into OutQuery4
select  avg(final) as price, category
from  MQ4_2
group by category;
```

Listing 1.5. NEXMark Query 4 template

```
select Istream(avg(Q.final))
from (select Rstream(max(B.price) as final, A.category)
        from Auction A [rows unbounded], Bid B [rows unbounded]
        where A.id=B.auction and B.dateTime < A.expires and
              A.expires < current_time
        group by A.id, A.category) Q
group by Q.category;
```

Results. Tables 4 and 5 contain the results from running NEXMark on Intel Xeon and RPI, respectively. In Queries 4–6, we distinguish between two versions: T stands for tumbling window, and S stands for sliding window. The SPEs run the benchmark on a single CPU core because the SPEs have a varying degree of concurrency support. An SPE like Flink is made for scalability, whereas the library versions of Esper and Siddhi are not. Kafka is used for communication between nodes in Flink and Beam, and therefore, also runs on a single core. The queries that cannot execute on the SPEs have empty table cells. Beam Flink means that Beam is executed with the Flink runner.

Flink performs the best among the SPEs in almost all queries, by a significant factor. One explanation might be that Flink has the most advanced processing environment out of all the SPEs. Flink's aggregation queries produce many fewer output tuples compared to the other SPEs, which positively affects the throughput. In contrast, Beam Flink has the worst performance in all cases. Beam Flink has a throughput between 6 and 73 times lower on the RPI, and between 2 and 11 times lower on the Intel Xeon server. These results seem to correspond with previous results from [11], in which Beam has a slowdown factor of between 4 and 58 times compared to Flink. The reason for the lower throughput might be a combination of overhead caused by Beam's attempt to be compatible with many SPEs and different policies regarding emission rate. However, more investigation is required to find out the reason why.

Noticeably, Queries 4 and 6 on Siddhi have a low throughput that is even higher on the RPI than the Intel Xeon server. The reason for the poor performance of those queries is that they perform joins on many tuples, with which Siddhi seems to perform poorly. Moreover, the Intel Xeon server uses a much larger dataset than the RPI. The first tuples require only around 2 microseconds processing time, but as the number of tuples in the windows increases, the final tuples require around 2.3 milliseconds of processing time each on the Intel Xeon server.

In Table 6, we scale the number of CPU cores that Flink and Kafka utilize and the number of queries deployed to Flink. The query is the same as Query 4 from the above tables. As we can see, the performance degrades much faster when running only one CPU core versus ten, as the number of queries increases. Even with one query deployed, running on multiple CPU cores increases the throughput from 110,900 tuples per second to 185,800 tuples per second. As the number of queries increases, the number of produced tuples also increases, which are forwarded to the sink node. Therefore, the throughput decreases for two reasons: the processing or networking capacity is overloaded.

Table 4. TPS and RSD when NEXMark runs on Intel Xeon five times.

Query	Beam Flink		Flink		Siddhi		T-Rex		Esper	
	TPS	RSD	TPS	RSD	TPS	RSD	TPS	RSD	TPS	RSD
0	26.3 k/s	0.69%	68.7 k/s	8%	34 k/s	0.51%	20.9 k/s	0.15%	29.4 k/s	0.61%
1	25.7 k/s	0.61%	68.6 k/s	7.7%	34.5 k/s	0.45%	–	–	32.4 k/s	0.84%
2	81.3 k/s	0.49%	197.6 k/s	6.2%	58.5 k/s	1.4%	–	–	46.8 k/s	1.5%
3	–	–	184 k/s	10.4%	56 k/s	1.4%	–	–	47.1 k/s	2.2%
4 (T)	–	–	–	.	585.7/s	0.62%	–	–	26.4 k/s	15.9%
4 (S)	–	–	103.6 k/s	6.8%	–	–	–	–	–	–
5 (T)	–	–	–	–	59.6 k/s	1.48%	–	–	30.2 k/s	16.8%
5 (S)	15.4 k/s	0.25%	107.8 k/s	11.6%	–	–	–	–	–	–
6 (T)	–	–	–	–	549.2/s	0.89%	–	–	30.9 k/s	20%
6 (S)	–	–	107.1 k/s	7.2%	–	–	–	–	–	–
7	12.7 k/s	0.2%	134.1 k/s	16.1%	59.3 k/s	1.2%	–	–	34.7 k/s	9.2%
8	–	–	184.4 k/s	16.5%	25.9 k/s	0.67%	–	–	47 k/s	3.6%

Table 5. TPS and RSD when NEXMark runs on an RPI five times.

Query	Beam Flink		Flink		Siddhi		T-Rex		Esper	
	TPS	RSD	TPS	RSD	TPS	RSD	TPS	RSD	TPS	RSD
0	679.9/s	1.6%	5 k/s	8.8%	3.9 k/s	0.44%	10.6 k/s	0.56%	2.8 k/s	0.8%
1	678.3/s	2.8%	4.1 k/s	8.1%	3.9 k/s	0.21%	–	–	2.9 k/s	0.47%
2	2.9 k/s	3.3%	28.3 k/s	5.4%	8 k/s	0.43%	–	–	7.6 k/s	0.77%
3	–	–	37.1 k/s	27.3%	7.7 k/s	0.88%	–	–	7.4 k/s	1.9%
4 (T)	–	–	–	–	2.1 k/s	0.98%	–	–	6.4 k/s	1.9%
4 (S)	–	–	10.8 k/s	13.5%	–	–	–	–	–	–
5 (T)	–	–	–	–	7.8 k/s	0.34%	–	–	6.5 k/s	6.1%
5 (S)	235.4/s	1.1%	9.8 k/s	16.6%	–	–	–	–	–	–
6 (T)	–	–	–	–	2.1 k/s	1.7%	–	–	5.7 k/s	6.7%
6 (S)	–	–	11.5 k/s	13%	–	–	–	–	–	–
7	236.2/s	1.2%	17.3 k/s	11.3%	7.5 k/s	0.65%	–	–	6.4 k/s	4.9%
8	–	–	34.6 k/s	22.5%	7.1 k/s	0.5%	–	–	7.1 k/s	1.8%

Table 6. TPS when Flink has deployed Query 4 from NEXMark and runs on Intel Xeon five times with a different number of CPU cores and queries.

# CPU cores	1 query	2 queries	5 queries	10 queries	15 queries	20 queries
1	110.9 k/s	73.3 k/s	36.3 k/s	18.8 k/s	13.2 k/s	9.3 k/s
10	185.8 k/s	177.3 k/s	134.2 k/s	63.5 k/s	47.7 k/s	28.3 k/s

4 Related Work

Few experiment frameworks for SPEs exist that aim at providing a user-friendly experience. The PEEL experiment framework is one of them [5]. It enables users to define experiments, execute them, and repeat them. Runtime logs from the running systems are collected, and so the experiments can be used to benchmark systems. However, they do not have a homogeneous input and output as we do. Their experiment definitions need special treatment for each SPE. Although the SPE-specific code for all SPEs is placed in the same experiment definition, it is not obvious that the SPEs will run the same tasks, as it is in our case. Moreover, their experiment definitions are programs written in Scala, which require significantly more effort than writing experiment definitions with Expose. Our result analysis is flexible with regard to the traced and varied parameters because of the tracing module that the SPEs must implement. In contrast, PEEL relies on the logs from the SPEs, making it harder for the SPEs to trace the same data.

FINCoS [20] is another experiment framework, which is an extended version of the benchmarking framework in [19]. They enable users to use their own datasets and can communicate with different SPE engines. However, it does not support automation of performance evaluations, which is a key feature of Expose. Moreover, since only Esper is mentioned to be supported, it is hard to determine the effort required to create a new "wrapper," whereas we have focused our efforts on simplifying this process. FINCoS does not appear to support arbitrary stream topologies; each node is either a data driver (data source), the SUT, or data sinks. Expose enables the experimenter to control the stream topology freely in the experiment. Nodes can be set to forward or redirect streams to an arbitrary number of nodes.

Multiple benchmarks and benchmark tools for stream processing exist in the literature [12,17]. One of the earliest works introduced is the Linear Road benchmark [3], which can be used to simulate traffic in motor highways. Systems may then achieve an L-rating that is a measure of their supported query load. Although Linear Road is relatively old, it is still implemented for new systems like Apache Flink [10], and for SPEs written in P4 for ASICS [15]. Other benchmarks include [7,12,16,18,21,22]. These benchmarks have in common that they are mainly meant for heavyweight SPEs such as Apache Storm, Apache Samza, Apache Spark and Apache Flink. In contrast, we consider the more lightweight SPEs that are relevant in fog networks and which might be sufficient for, e.g., Internet of Things applications.

The unification of the use of SPE systems is an ongoing effort. A Stream SQL standard is recently proposed in [4] and is in the process of being implemented for existing SPEs. Apache Beam is a framework that attempts to unify SPEs by providing a unified interface for writing SPE applications. It performs a task similar to Expose in that Expose unifies the definition and execution of distributed experiments, and Beam unifies the execution model of the SPEs.

5   Conclusion

We present in this work a framework that simplifies the definition and execution of distributed SPE experiments. A set of experiments can be defined in an experiment definition file, and the same experiment definition can be used to execute different SPEs, which makes comparisons of multiple SPEs easier. Combined with our design choice that experts implement the SPE wrappers and the fact that we add only a very thin software layer on top of the SPEs, Expose achieves fair treatment of SPEs. This prevents bias from experimenters that are experts in one class of SPEs and novices in others.

To demonstrate the ease with which experiments can be defined and executed, we create an experiment definition that describes a well-known benchmark called NEXMark using Expose. Then we run it with Flink, Beam Flink, Siddhi, T-Rex, and Esper on a powerful server and a resource-constrained Raspberry Pi 4. The experiment definition is concise, reusable, and can be changed by a user to suit their particular needs.

For future work, we aim at adding the ability to decentralize the coordination of nodes, which means that nodes can issue tasks to other nodes. That way, we can test out time-critical algorithms and variations between them. An example of this is operator migration algorithms in distributed CEP. For that to be possible, the SPE wrappers must be extended with more tasks, such as the ability to move query state between nodes and stopping and buffering streams.

References

1. Apache Beam. https://beam.apache.org. Accessed 6 Aug 2020
2. Esper. http://www.espertech.com/esper. Accessed 6 Aug 2020
3. Arasu, A., et al.: Linear road: a stream data management benchmark. In: Proceedings of the Thirtieth international Conference on Very Large Data Bases, vol. 30. pp. 480–491. VLDB Endowment (2004)
4. Begoli, E., Akidau, T., Hueske, F., Hyde, J., Knight, K., Knowles, K.: One SQL to rule them all-an efficient and syntactically idiomatic approach to management of streams and tables. In: Proceedings of the 2019 International Conference on Management of Data, pp. 1757–1772 (2019)
5. Boden, C., Alexandrov, A., Kunft, A., Rabl, T., Markl, V.: PEEL: a framework for benchmarking distributed systems and algorithms. In: Nambiar, R., Poess, M. (eds.) TPCTC 2017. LNCS, vol. 10661, pp. 9–24. Springer, Cham (2018). https://doi.org/10.1007/978-3-319-72401-0_2
6. Carbone, P., Katsifodimos, A., Ewen, S., Markl, V., Haridi, S., Tzoumas, K.: Apache Flink: Stream and batch processing in a single engine. In: Bulletin of the IEEE Computer Society Technical Committee on Data Engineering, vol. 36, no. 4 (2015)
7. Chintapalli, S., et al.: Benchmarking streaming computation engines: Storm, Flink and Spark streaming. In: 2016 IEEE international parallel and distributed processing symposium workshops (IPDPSW), pp. 1789–1792. IEEE (2016)
8. Cugola, G., Margara, A.: Complex event processing with T-REX. J. Syst. Softw. **85**(8), 1709–1728 (2012)

9. Folkerts, E., Alexandrov, A., Sachs, K., Iosup, A., Markl, V., Tosun, C.: Benchmarking in the cloud: what it should, can, and cannot be. In: Nambiar, R., Poess, M. (eds.) TPCTC 2012. LNCS, vol. 7755, pp. 173–188. Springer, Heidelberg (2013). https://doi.org/10.1007/978-3-642-36727-4_12

10. Hanif, M., Yoon, H., Lee, C.: Benchmarking tool for modern distributed stream processing engines. In: 2019 International Conference on Information Networking (ICOIN), pp. 393–395. IEEE (2019)

11. Hesse, G., Matthies, C., Glass, K., Huegle, J., Uflacker, M.: Quantitative impact evaluation of an abstraction layer for data stream processing systems. In: 2019 IEEE 39th International Conference on Distributed Computing Systems (ICDCS), pp. 1381–1392. IEEE (2019)

12. Hesse, G., Reissaus, B., Matthies, C., Lorenz, M., Kraus, M., Uflacker, M.: Senska – towards an enterprise streaming benchmark. In: Nambiar, R., Poess, M. (eds.) TPCTC 2017. LNCS, vol. 10661, pp. 25–40. Springer, Cham (2018). https://doi.org/10.1007/978-3-319-72401-0_3

13. Hochstein, L., Moser, R.: Ansible: Up and Running: Automating Configuration Management and Deployment the Easy Way. O'Reilly Media Inc, Sebastopol (2017)

14. Huppler, K.: The art of building a good benchmark. In: Nambiar, R., Poess, M. (eds.) Performance Evaluation and Benchmarking. TPCTC 2009. LNCS, vol. 5895, pp. 18–30. Springer, Heidelberg (2009). https://doi.org/10.1007/978-3-642-10424-4_3

15. Jepsen, T., Moshref, M., Carzaniga, A., Foster, N., Soulé, R.: Life in the fast lane: A line-rate linear road. In: Proceedings of the Symposium on SDN Research, pp. 1–7 (2018)

16. Karimov, J., Rabl, T., Katsifodimos, A., Samarev, R., Heiskanen, H., Markl, V.: Benchmarking distributed stream data processing systems. In: 2018 IEEE 34th International Conference on Data Engineering (ICDE), pp. 1507–1518. IEEE (2018)

17. Kiatipis, A., et al.: A survey of benchmarks to evaluate data analytics for smart-* applications. arXiv preprint arXiv:1910.02004 (2019)

18. Lu, R., Wu, G., Xie, B., Hu, J.: Stream bench: towards benchmarking modern distributed stream computing frameworks. In: 2014 IEEE/ACM 7th International Conference on Utility and Cloud Computing, pp. 69–78. IEEE (2014)

19. Mendes, M.R., Bizarro, P., Marques, P.: A framework for performance evaluation of complex event processing systems. In: Proceedings of the Second International Conference on Distributed Event-Based Systems, pp. 313–316 (2008)

20. Mendes, M.R., Bizarro, P., Marques, P.: Fincos: benchmark tools for event processing systems. In: Proceedings of the 4th ACM/SPEC International Conference on Performance Engineering, pp. 431–432 (2013)

21. Rabl, T., Frank, M., Danisch, M., Jacobsen, H.A., Gowda, B.: The vision of bigbench 2.0. In: Proceedings of the Fourth Workshop on Data analytics in the Cloud, pp. 1–4 (2015)

22. Shukla, A., Chaturvedi, S., Simmhan, Y.: RioTBench: an IoT benchmark for distributed stream processing systems. Concurrency Comput. Pract. Exp. **29**(21), e4257 (2017)

23. Stonebraker, M., Çetintemel, U.: "One size fits all" an idea whose time has come and gone. In: Making Databases Work: The Pragmatic Wisdom of Michael Stonebraker, pp. 441–462 (2018)

24. Suhothayan, S., Gajasinghe, K., Loku Narangoda, I., Chaturanga, S., Perera, S., Nanayakkara, V.: Siddhi: a second look at complex event processing architectures. In: Proceedings of the 2011 ACM workshop on Gateway Computing Environments, pp. 43–50 (2011)
25. Tucker, P., Tufte, K., Papadimos, V., Maier, D.: NEXMark-a benchmark for queries over data streams (draft). OGI School of Science & Engineering at OHSU, September, Technical report (2008)

Revisiting Issues in Benchmark Metric Selection

Christopher Elford, Dippy Aggarwal$^{(\boxtimes)}$, and Shreyas Shekhar

Intel Corporation, Santa Clara, USA
{chris.l.elford,dippy.aggarwal,shreyas.shekhar}@intel.com

Abstract. In 1986, Fleming and Wallace presented a case advocating the use of geomean in benchmark results. 23 years later in 2009, Alain Crolotte followed up on that proposal at TPCTC using TPC-D as a reference. Now 11 years later it is time to present another perspective on the age-old argument regarding the best metric for summarizing benchmark data. The aim of this paper is two-fold: (1) summarize the definition and interpretation of the current benchmark metrics for the OLAP family of the TPC benchmarks, including TPC-H, TPC-DS, and TPCx-BB. (2) illustrate the impact and tradeoffs of different statistical measures on the overall benchmark metric score, using both conceptual and data-driven arguments. Our hope is that the paper reinvigorates interest in the benchmark community to re-evaluate the design of benchmark metrics and offer insights that can influence the future direction of benchmark metrics design.

Keywords: Benchmarks · Databases · Performance · Metrics

1 Introduction

Database benchmarking is a valuable process that measures combined performance of various components of a database engine along with the underlying hardware. The investment of time and money is motivated by the desire to identify areas for optimizations and to demonstrate one's standing against competition in the market. As laid out by Peter Mattson, General Chair of MLPerf, "Benchmarking aligns research with development, engineering with marketing, and competitors across the industry in pursuit of a clear objective [1]."

TPC [21] (Transaction Processing Performance Council), a consortium led by a committee of industry and academic experts, is responsible for developing, managing, and auditing several database benchmarks spanning the areas of analytics, big data, transaction processing, IoT, and AI. This paper focuses specifically on the three analytical/Big Data benchmarks provided by TPC: TPC-H [2], TPC-DS [3], and TPCx-BB [4].

One of the key challenges in developing a database benchmark is the definition of a composite benchmark metric which serves as an objective criteria/score for database vendors and system designers to evaluate and compare

© Springer Nature Switzerland AG 2021
R. Nambiar and M. Poess (Eds.): TPCTC 2020, LNCS 12752, pp. 35–47, 2021.
https://doi.org/10.1007/978-3-030-84924-5_3

their products against competitors. The metric captures end to end database performance by combining individual performance and interactions of different scenarios/phases such as data load, power run (simulating a single user test with all queries in the benchmark run in a sequential order), throughput run (multiple query streams running concurrently), and others. The performance of these individual phases is combined in specific ratios using different statistical measures such as arithmetic or geometric mean and the choice of a particular statistic influences database vendor's decision for where to focus their efforts to drive performance optimizations and hence have the highest impact on the benchmark metric score.

While we cover the implications of employing arithmetic vs. geometric mean in the context of benchmark metric later in the paper (Sect. 2), we discuss them briefly here. Using arithmetic mean to summarize the performance (runtime) of the power run of a benchmark implies that optimizing only the few top running queries is enough to boost the benchmark score while ignoring the short running queries since the higher execution times will skew the average towards them. However, geometric mean by its definition offers equal weightage to all queries.

There have been discussions in the past which highlight the design reasons that have led to the current metric definitions of some of the performance benchmarks [5,6,8,10,12]. In 1986, Fleming and Wallace [6] proved that geometric mean is the only correct average of normalized measurements. Fast forward 20 years, Crolotte [5] proved that arithmetic mean is the only valid metric to summarize single-stream elapsed times for decision-support benchmark. Crolotte cited pitfalls from using geomean in TPC-D to motivate the omission of geomean in TPC-DS which is based on TPC-D. Nambiar et al. [8] justify their choice of using arithmetic mean for the power run component of TPC-DS benchmark by highlighting that more real world customer scenarios are around optimizing long running queries. Citron et al. [12] conducted an interesting analysis around the topic of appropriate mean for comparing multi-workload groups of metrics to each other based on a literature survey and their independent experiments. The authors observe that the "best" choice of statistical average fluctuates widely from changing even a single ingredient workload in the group. They conclude that relative computer performance cannot be assessed in an absolute manner by a small number of contrasting or toy benchmarks regardless of the choice of statistical average. John [10] presents a case for weighted average. As another independent observation derived from reviewing of the current TPC-DS publications, longest query accounts for 7.6% of the power run time but 12.5% of the Throughput runtime. This presents another argument in favor of focusing the optimization efforts on the top long running queries since that will have an even larger impact on the throughput metric as well. Literature survey on the topic of benchmark metrics is replete with arguments favoring the use of one mean vs. other [9,11].

McChesney [13] and Mashey [9,11] provides a primer on the relationship between lognormal data and geometric means. Recently, in a journal (Communications in Statistics - Theory and Practice), Vogel summarized the deep history of a number of data distributions and ways to summarize central tendency across multiple disciplines. It also supports the premise that there is a relationship between lognormal data and the geometric mean.

Our motivation to revive this discussion comes from following three observations: (1) TPC-DS consists of 99 queries and by using arithmetic mean to summarize the results from complete run of these 99 queries, we believe that we are not only steering the attention of database vendors to a handul of top running queries but it also begs the question for why do we need the rest of queries in the benchmark if performance optimizations around them are not effectively counted towards benchmark score. (2) Literature has numerous examples of using geomean for lognormal data and interestingly, TPC-DS does reflect lognormal distribution [11] (details in Sect. 3). (3) While TPC-DS consists of 99 queries representative of industry operations, not all 99 queries would necessarily be relevant to all end users. If a long running query is irrelevant to a given end user the metric is of limited utility.

Through this paper, we hope to revive the discussion and present our observations highlighting limitations in the current definition of the TPC-DS metric which is based on using arithmetic means to capture results of the power run phase of the benchmark. We raise the following questions, answers to which will lay the foundation for our ideas in this paper.

1. What constitutes the objective criteria/benchmark metric? How do the current metrics of TPC ad-hoc query benchmarks compare?
2. Analyze the impact and tradeoffs of different statistical measures on the benchmark metric score. Is the Benchmark Metric "Reward Structure" for the newer benchmarks better than the earlier benchmarks?
3. How hard is it to design a metric that "fairly" rewards optimization? What influences the constituent mix of a benchmark metric?

We address the first two questions in detail in Sect. 2 and the challenges and pros and cons of different metric designs is covered in Sect. 3. Based on the recognized issues, we then leverage the discussion to present our proposal of considering the use of geomean for computing the performance of the power run component of TPC-DS. Section 4 summarizes our ideas along with enumeration of questions that must be addressed for the successful implementation of our proposal of employing geomean for TPC-DS power run phase.

Before moving forward with the discussion, below are the definitions of the various terms that will reoccur throughout the paper and represent key ingredients used in defining the metric.

1. *Benchmark "Reward Structure"*: How much does the benchmark score improve on optimizing a system ingredient?
2. *Power Run*: A single series of queries run one at a time (in a defined order)
3. *Throughput Run*: Several concurrent series of queries run together (each series in a defined order)
4. *Load*: Creation of the database (includes population, indexing, etc.)
5. *Maintenance*: Updating [refreshing] database with a [partial] fresh data snapshot
6. *Scale Factor*: Any of a series of discrete allowed database sizes

2   Survey of TPC OLAP/Big Data Metrics

In this section, we analyze the characteristics of three analytical benchmarks offered by TPC: TPC-H, TPC-DS, and TPCx-BB, focusing on both their commonalities and differences (e.g., the presence of a data maintainence phase in TPC-H and TPC-DS which is not a part of TPCx-BB) and comparing their respective benchmark metrics. All the three benchmarks involve running power and throughput run phases. We draw interpretations of these benchmark metrics to highlight the design rationale behind each of them and how the they steer system's and database vendors attention to optimize certain phases of their products.

2.1   TPC-H

TPC-H has been the most popular and widely embraced analytical benchmark across both academic research (7500+ results for TPC-H in google scholar [14]) and industry practitioners (290+ publications [15]). It is a decision-support benchmark which analyzes large volumes of data to answer ad-hoc queries representing business critical scenarios such as pricing summary report which captures the amount of business that was billed, shipped, or returned. A TPC-H performance metric (Queries per hour - Qph) for a given Scale factor (SF) consists of two geometrically equal weighted phases:

1. Power@Size is the combined duration of 22 sequential queries and two refresh queries. The queries are given geometrically equal weights. $Q(i,0)$ in the second equation represents read only queries while $R(j,0)$ correspond to the two refresh queries.

$$QphH@Size = \sqrt{Power@Size * Throughput@Size} \qquad (1)$$

$$TPC-HPower@Size = \frac{3600 * SF}{\sqrt[24]{\prod_{i=1}^{i=22} Q(i,0) * \prod_{j=1}^{j=2} R(j,0)}} \qquad (2)$$

2. Throughput@Size is the combined duration of multiple simultaneous streams of 22 queries (and their associated refreshes).

   Interpretation
   The metric definition above can be interpreted as follows.
1. There is no need to optimize database load time in TPC-H.
2. There is no bias toward optimizing data maintenance (update queries) any more or less than the read only analytics queries.

In the next section, we do a similar analysis of the metric design of another TPC benchmark, TPC-DS which is gaining popularity over the past few years since it supersedes TPC-H in terms of schema complexity and the query coverage (99 queries in TPC-DS vs. 22 in TPC-H) [8].

2.2 TPC-DS

TPC-DS exhibits several commonalities with TPC-H given that both are decision support, analytical benchmarks. They have several phases in common including power run, throughput run, and data maintainence but there also exists key areas where it diverges from the TPC-H benchmark design. The throughput run in TPC-DS is run twice, once immediately after the power run and once after data maintainence. The TPC-DS performance metric significantly differs from TPC-H in that for a given scale factor (SF) consists of four geometricly equal weighted phases:

1. Power (T_{PT}) is the combined duration of 99 sequential queries. The value is multipled by the stream count to place it into a similar scale as the Throughput timing.
2. Throughput (T_{TT}) is the combined duration of multiple simultaneous streams of 99 queries running twice.
3. Maintenance (T_{DM}) is the time to perform data maintenance (update queries) which is run in two phases.
4. Load (T_{LD}) is the time to load the database, configure indices, etc. It constitutes one percent of the duration multipled by the stream count, S_{CT}.

$$QphDS@SF = \frac{SF * S_{CT} * 99}{\sqrt[4]{T_{PT} * T_{TT} * T_{DM} * T_{LD}}} \qquad (3)$$

Interpretation

1. Because a geomean is used to combine the four phases, ingredient providers are encouraged to equally optimize for all four activities (single-stream, multi-stream, data updates, load efficiency). For example, given a choice between improving single stream performance by 10%, multiple stream performance by 10%, data maintenance by 10%, or data load by 10%, all would provide an equal bump to the benchmark metric.
2. Within the power metric, total time is used which rewards the provider from optimizing the longest running queries and minimizes benefits from optimizing shorter running queries. This begs the question of why TPC-DS includes all 99 queries.
3. While the power run metric and throughput components of TPC-H include both read-only and refresh queries, TPC-DS incorporates refresh queries in a separate phase (T_{DM}) and accounts for only 99 read-only queries for the power and throughput run components of its metrics (T_{PT}, T_{TT}).

The use of arithmetic mean vs. geometric mean in the TPC-H and TPC-DS metrics respectively for the power run brings back the historical controversary: *is it really desirable to give an equal benefit to the benchmark score from improving a short running query and a long running query?* For example, the use of geometric mean in TPC-H (Eq. 2) offers equal weightage to a 10% optimization observed over a long running query vs. a short running one whereas the arithmetic mean used in TPC-DS favors optimizations to long running queries.

In the next section, we cover yet another TPC benchmark, TPCx-BB which is an analytical benchmark like TPC-H and TPC-DS but extends the workload beyond the traditional, structured data supported by TPC-H and TPC-DS.

2.3   TPCx-BB

TPCx-BB extends the previous analytical benchmarks by integrating machine learning and natural language processing queries as well alongside SQL queries on structured data. The scale of supported database sizes in TPCx-BB is also higher (1 PB) compared to H/DS (100 TB). A TPCx-BB performance metric consists of two geometrically equal weighted phases coupled with a portion of the load time.

1. T_{LD} is 10% of the load time.
2. T_{PT} is computed much like TPC-H with a geomean of the 30 TPCx-BB query durations.
3. T_{TT} is computed much like TPC-H with a net time of multiple streams running simultaneously.

$$BBQpm@SF = \frac{SF * 60 * 30}{T_{LD} + \sqrt[2]{T_{PT} * T_{TT}}} \tag{4}$$

$$T_{PT} = 30 * \sqrt[30]{\prod_{i=1}^{i=30} Q(i,0)} \tag{5}$$

Interpretation

1. Unlike TPC-H and TPC-DS, the current generation of TPCx-BB has no refresh queries to include in the metric.
2. Because only 10% of the load time is accounted for in the metric, the load time needs to be significantly longer than the power/throughput run time before load time optimization is justified.

While this section provided a conceptual and formula based interpretation of the current metrics, in the next section we present a quantitative evidence for the interpretations drawn above for each of the benchmark metrics.

2.4   Survey Summary

We now illustrate how the optimizations over different benchmark phases impact the benchmark metric using actual numbers from published reports on each of the three benchmarks. We took a current TPC-H [16], TPC-DS [17], and TPCx-BB [18] publication, and their associated Load, Query, and Refresh times. We then artificially adjusted by 10% their load times, refresh times, power run and throughput run query times, and their longest and shortest query times. For simplicity, for the longest and shortest query time adjustment, we reduced the respective query duration in both the power and in the throughput runs. This is likely a conservative estimate for the impact on the Throughput Run because interaction effects will likely inflate times in queries running in parallel in other streams.

We then recomputed a theoretical benchmark score based on the adjusted times. In the table below (Table 1) we show the impact to overall score from a theoretical 10% optimization to each portion of the benchmark described as follows. The first row in the table serves as the baseline.

- *Load 10% faster*: Adapts the load time to 90% of the original time listed in the publication.
- *All RF Queries 10% faster*: Computes the benchmark score by revising the runtime of each of the refresh queries to 90% of their original runtimes in the publication.
- *All Power/Throughput Run Queries 10% faster*: Computes the benchmark score by revising the runtime of all power and throughput run queries to 90% of their original runtimes in the publication.
- *All Power Run Queries 10% faster*: Computes the benchmark score by revising the runtime of all power run queries to 90% of their original runtimes in the publication.
- *All Throughput Run Queries 10% faster*: Computes the benchmark score by revising the runtime of all throughput run queries to 90% of their original runtimes in the publication.

Table 1. TPC-H, TPC-DS, TPCx-BB optimization reward structure

Row#	Workload element	TPC-H	TPC-DS	TPCx-BB
1	Base	100.0%	100.0%	100.0%
2	Load 10% faster	na	102.7%	100.5%
3	All RF queries 10% faster	100.4%	102.7%	n/a
4	All power/throughput run queries 10% faster	110.6%	105.4%	110.5%
5	All power run queries 10% faster	104.9%	102.7%	105.1%
6	All throughput run queries 10% faster	105.4%	102.7%	105.1%
7	Longest query 10% faster	100.6%	100.5%	101.4%
8	Shortest query 10% faster	100.2%	100.0%	100.2%

Observations

1. As shown in Table 1 , the three workloads intentionally or unintentionally reward/place very different importance on data load and data maintenance (Rows 2,3). In contrast to TPC-H, TPC-DS dramatically increases the importance of optimizing the load and refresh phases; giving them equal metric impact as the power and throughput runs (Rows 5,6). In practice, some end

users may heavily stress data load time by frequently refreshing data sets while other users may only infrequently reload their data sets. Similarly some users will heavily rely on data maintenance while others may not.

2. With respect to an across the board optimization of all queries in the power and/or throughput run phases (Rows 4–6), Table 1 shows that all three TPC benchmarks agree and actively try to provide reward to optimizing whole benchmark phases. But the award percentage in TPC-DS (105.4%) is almost half compared to the incentive provided in TPC-H and TPCx-BB (110.6% and 110.5% in TPC-H and TPCx-BB respectively). In practice, some users may stress a single query at a time while other users stress multiple concurrent queries.

3. As expected, TPC-H significantly rewards optimization of the whole power or throughput run phase (Rows 4–6), gives a reasonable reward to optimizing the longest running query (Row 7), and gives a tiny reward to optimizing refresh queries (Row 3) or the shortest running query (Row 8).

4. TPC-DS maintains TPC-H's reasonable reward granted to optimizing the longest running query but gives essentially no benefit to optimizing the shortest running queries (Row 8).

5. TPCx-BB is similar to TPC-H with significant rewards to optimizing the whole power or throughput run phase, a modest reward to optimizing the longest running query, and a tiny reward to optimizing the shortest running query.

In summary, TPC-H and TPCx-BB both recognize that the short running queries still play an important role and use a geomean which prevents them being completely ignored. In contrast, the design of the TPC-DS metric encourages the short running queries to be ignored during optimization. This is ironic given that one of the interesting claims to fame of TPC-DS is that it dramatically increases the count of real-world user query types relative to workloads like its TPC-H predecessor. However, the number of queries that actually make a significant difference to the metric may not be nearly as large in TPC-DS.

For all three of these benchmarks, TPC and its members invested years of engineering effort to identify a variety of real world ad-hoc queries that represent the types of queries performed in decision support and big data production environments. Having closed on a set of queries, each benchmark formed a metric that encourages test sponsors to optimize selected elements of the solution. We posit that all three benchmarks contain limitations or implicit assumptions in their selection and will discuss it in the next section as it relates to each of the thought experiments in Table 1 above.

3   Metric Design Considerations

Fleming and Wallace [6] passionately argue for geomean for summarizing normalized results and provides a proof based on certain assumptions that geomean is decidedly better. Crolotte [5] argues with equal passion for arithmetic mean and provides a similar proof based on alternate assumptions that arithmetic mean is decisively better. He also provides an interesting example outlining how the choice of metric contributed to the early demise of TPC-D. Our argument for a choice of metric while no less passionate is conceptually based on how TPC benchmarks are designed.

The choice of metric fundamentally guides the one publishing the benchmark towards system ingredients that should be optimized to achieve higher scores. In Sects. 1 and 2, we compared and contrasted the ingredients that are encouraged for optimization in the TPC-H, TPC-DS, and TPCx-BB benchmarks. In this section, we lay the foundation for our proposal to consider geometric mean and its variations in defining the power run component of the TPC-DS metric.

3.1   Ideal Metric and Challenges

From the perspective of an end user downloading a TPC benchmark result and its disclosure and trying to understand how to use the result in their decisions on how to provision their environment, the answer is fairly simple: *The end user would like a metric that rewards the particular queries that the user tends to use in* **their** *environment highly and ignores the remaining queries.* If, for example, those happen to all be short running queries then the short running queries should be highly rewarded. The perspective that different end users may stress different queries highlights the fact that there are challenges inherent in defining an ideal benchmark metric that can serve the use cases for different database vendors and system designers without incurring any bias. We recognize the following specific challenges in the design of an ideal benchmark metric.

1. Since each user may have a different set of queries that they are interested in, it is practically impossible to create a single metric that reflects all combinations. All three benchmarks largely ignore the relative frequency of the queries.
2. Since there are dependencies amongst the queries such as earlier queries loading data that will then be used by later queries and more complex interaction effects between streams in the Throughput run, it is impossible in the general case to reliably extract timing for one or two queries from a TPC benchmark run and assume that they would represent the performance of those queries in isolation.
3. A savvy user can create a metric using data extracted from TPC benchmarks that represents their environment but that representation may or may not be an adequate substitute for actually running the query mix that they are interested in situ.

3.2   Candidate Solutions

We offer two proposals for revising the TPC-DS power run metric subcomponent in the overall benchmark score.

Using Geometric Mean Instead of Arithmetic Mean: For this option, we will posit a variant of TPC-DS that equally rewards a given percentage speedup to each query independent of its power duration (similar to TPC-H and TPCx-BB). Note the difference in the revised power run metric component in Eq. 7 (geomean) compared to T_{PT} described in Sect. 2.2.

$$GphDS@SF = \frac{SF * S_{CT} * 99}{\sqrt[4]{G_{PT} * T_{TT} * T_{DM} * T_{LD}}} \tag{6}$$

where

$$G_{PT} = S_{CT} * 99 * \sqrt[99]{\prod_{i=1}^{i=99} Q(i,0)} \tag{7}$$

[7,11,13] posit that data of a lognormal distribution tends to be best summarized via a geomean. Despite the concerns of [5], the authors of this paper believe that the geomean has an important role to play to ensure that short and long queries each can play their role within the benchmark and can serve as an alternative to a weighted mean when it is "too hard" to agree on relative query weights. In Figs. 1a and 1b we show two TPC-DS publications [19,20] which are randomly chosen from the available publication results. The bell shaped graphs confirm how the power run query times are indeed lognormal further supporting the position that geomean does have a role to play if we want to reflect queries across the spectrum.

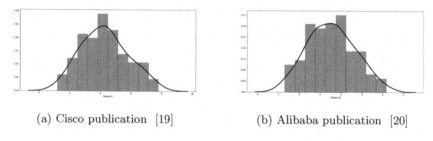

(a) Cisco publication [19]   (b) Alibaba publication [20]

Fig. 1. Demonstrating lognormal characteristic of TPC-DS

Using Weighted Geometric Mean Instead of Arithmetic/Pure Geometric Mean: For this second option, we will provide some targeted weighting to give a larger reward for optimizing certain queries over others. While all three benchmarks contain a number of real world representative ad-hoc query use cases, none of the three benchmarks define the real-world relative frequency of each query. If they did, a weighted average could be used to accurately reflect the importance of the queries. As an example, if a short running query in practice is run 1,000,000 times more often than a long running query it could be realistically accounted for in the metric. Unfortunately agreeing on the frequency of execution of all the query types within the TPC benchmark development committees would be an even harder process than agreeing on the list of queries to include in the first place. We discuss this further in Sect. 4.

$$WGphDS@SF = \frac{SF * S_{CT} * 99}{\sqrt[4]{WG_{PT} * T_{TT} * T_{DM} * T_{LD}}} \tag{8}$$

where

$$WG_{PT} = S_{CT} * 99 * {}^{\sum_{j=1}^{n} w_j}\sqrt{\prod_{i=1}^{i=99} Q(i,0)^{w_i}} \tag{9}$$

Table 2 shows the results of applying these alternative metric schemes (geomean and weighted geomean) to the TPC-DS benchmark score. For discussion, we will maintain the current TPC-DS award structure as is and assume that in the prescence of an across the board optimization to all queries in the power and/or throughput run it should gain a similar benchmark score boost. We refer to the query runtimes from the same TPC-DS publication [17] that was referenced for results shown in Table 1 but instead of using an arithmetic mean, we use alternative metrics in Table 2.

Table 2. Demonstrating experimental optimization reward structure

Workload element	Current metric	Pure Geomean	Weighted Geomean
Base	100.00%	100.00%	100.00%
Load 10% faster	102.67%	102.67%	102.67%
All RF queries 10% faster	102.67%	102.67%	102.67%
All power/throughput run queries 10% faster	105.41%	105.41%	105.41%
All power run queries 10% faster	102.67%	102.67%	102.67%
All throughput run queries 10% faster	102.67%	102.67%	102.67%
Longest query 10% faster	100.47%	100.31%	100.29%
Shortest query 10% faster	100.00%	100.03%	100.04%

In the current metric (Column 2), we recognize that while a 10% optimization on the longest query is able to improve the score to 100.47% but the same amount of optimization over the shortest running query shows no improvement to the overall score. Leveraging geomean (Column 3) instead helps to alleviate that skew by offering some small incentive to optimizations on short running queries as well (100.03%) by slightly reducing the impact of long running queries. but the relative impact of the long running queries is still quite high. The weighted geomean in the Column 4 illustrates an approach to balance this further by offering a higher reward to the short running queries. While actual query weights should be determined by the committee, for the sake of discussion of the impact of a weighted geomean we use an arbitrary scenario that gives 4× weight to the the shortest running 25 queries. Further adjusting the weights could produce a more significant adjustment as desired.

4   Conclusions and Next Steps

This concludes our discussion around the issues, tradeoffs, and potential improvements in the benchmark metrics design. We summarized the definition and interpretation of the current benchmark metrics for the OLAP family of the TPC benchmarks, including TPC-H, TPC-DS, and TPCx-BB. Using that as the foundation, we illustrated the impact and tradeoffs of different statistical measures on the overall benchmark metric score, using both conceptual and data-driven arguments. While the two TPC analytical benchmarks, TPC-H and TPCx-BB employ a geometric mean to summarize the impact of power run on the overall benchmark score, TPC-DS uses an arithmetic mean. Our results demonstrate how a weighted geometric mean can offer additional control for defining the benchmark metric as opposed to arithmetic or geometric means which are either skewed towards long running queries or completely eliminate any ranking among the queries in terms of their respective runtimes.

As the next step, we would like to invite the TPC committee, industry leaders and practitioners in the field of performance engineering and benchmarking to consider re-evaluating the reward structure used in the design of benchmark metrics . Some of the aspects to consider are:

1. Which queries should have the largest reward?
2. Which phases should impact benchmark score the most?
3. Should TPC-DS 3.0 incorporate a weighted geomean? If so, how should the query weights be defined (e.g., query frequency, query duration, resource use such as CPU/IO, etc.).

Having presented these ideas for future discussions, we also recognize the complexity involved in implementing concrete solutions. To address the challenge, one of the steps can be to turn our attention back to the fundamental question that forms the basis of this discussion of the relevant statistical measure for a benchmark metric. The question being, *what are the goals that the benchmark designers seek to achieve and how does the current choice of metrics (and underlying statistical measures) help those goals?* We believe there are two main expectations.

1. The metric offer insights to the database and system designers on where to focus their optimization efforts to improve their benchmark scores.
2. As a benchmark designer, we want to steer the vendors' attention to areas that will improve end user experience and solve real challenges in the industry.

The choice of statistical measures in the existing metrics is based solely on the query runtimes. The arithmetic mean focuses one's efforts primarily on optimizing the "long" running queries while geomean offers equal incentives towards all queries. We believe that in our discussion around this area, we should look beyond query runtimes to include the aspect of representativeness of the query (e.g., based on either its frequency of use or some other resource usage) in the real-world customer uses cases. One opportunity for future work is to create a taxonomy regarding resource types suitable for inclusion in weighting decisions.

We hope that bringing forth and reviving this discussion around benchmark metrics selection serves as a worthwhile effort to not only ensure that TPC benchmarks continue to offer valuable insights to customers and database and system designers alike but also address how we can make end users more inclined to embrace results.

References

1. ML Benchmark Design Challenges - Hot Chips. https://www.hotchips.org/hc31/HC31_1.9_MethodologyAndMLSystem-MLPerf-rev-b.pdf. Accessed 14 Sept 2020
2. TPC-H. http://www.tpc.org/tpch/default5.asp. Accessed 14 Sept 2020
3. TPC-DS. http://www.tpc.org/tpcds/default5.asp. Accessed 14 Sept 2020
4. TPCx-BB. http://www.tpc.org/tpcx-bb/default5.asp. Accessed 14 Sept 2020
5. Crolotte, A.: Issues in benchmark metric selection. In: Nambiar, R., Poess, M. (eds.) TPCTC 2009. LNCS, vol. 5895, pp. 146–152. Springer, Heidelberg (2009). https://doi.org/10.1007/978-3-642-10424-4_11
6. Fleming, P.J., Wallace, J.J.: How not to lie with statistics: the correct way to summarize benchmark results. Commun. ACM **29**(3), 218–221 (1986)
7. Vogel, R.M.: The geometric mean?. Commun. Stat. Theor. Methods 1–13 (2020)
8. Nambiar, R.O., Poess, M.: The Making of TPC-DS. In: VLDB, vol. 6, pp. 1049–1058 (2006)
9. Mashey, J.R.: War of the benchmark means: time for a truce. ACM SIGARCH Comput. Archit. News **32**(4), 1–14 (2004)
10. John, LK.: More on finding a single number to indicate overall performance of a benchmark suite. ACM SIGARCH Comput. Archit. News **32**(1), 3–8 (2004)
11. Iqbal, M.F., John, L.K.: Confusion by all means. In: Proceedings of the 6th International Workshop on Unique Chips and Systems (UCAS-6). (2010)
12. Citron, D., Hurani, A., Gnadrey, A.: The harmonic or geometric mean: does it really matter? ACM SIGARCH Comput. Archit. News **34**(4), 18–25 (2006)
13. Three simple statistics for your data visualizations. https://breakforsense.net/three-statistics/. Accessed 14 Sept 2020
14. TPC-H Google Scholar Search Results. https://scholar.google.com/scholar?as_vis=1&q=tpc-h+&hl=en&as_sdt=1,48. Accessed 14 Sept 2020
15. TPC-H Results. http://www.tpc.org/tpch/results/tpch_advanced_sort5.asp?PRINTVER=false&FLTCOL1=ALL&ADDFILTERROW=&filterRowCount=1&SRTCOL1=h_sponsor&SRTDIR1=ASC&ADDSORTROW=&sortRowCount=1&DISPRES=100+PERCENT&include_withdrawn_results=none&include_historic_results=yes. Accessed 14 Sept 2020
16. TPC-H Publication. http://www.tpc.org/tpch/results/tpch_result_detail5.asp?id=119040201. Accessed 14 Sept 2020
17. TPC-DS Publication. http://www.tpc.org/tpcds/results/tpcds_result_detail5.asp?id=120061701. Accessed 14 Sept 2020
18. TPCx-BB Publication. http://www.tpc.org/tpcx-bb/results/tpcxbb_result_detail5.asp?id=119101101. Accessed 14 Sept 2020
19. Cisco UCS Integrated Infrastructure for Big Data. http://www.tpc.org/tpcds/results/tpcds_result_detail5.asp?id=118030501. Accessed 14 Sept 2020
20. Alibaba Cloud AnalyticDB. http://www.tpc.org/tpcds/results/tpcds_result_detail5.asp?id=120061701. Accessed 14 Sept 2020
21. TPC. http://www.tpc.org. Accessed 15 Sept 2020

Performance Evaluation for Digital Transformation

Suresh Gopalakrishnan[✉]

"Purposeful Digital Transformation", Santa Clara, CA, USA
suresh@sureshg.com

Abstract. We live in the digital age where consumer experiences are driving our expectations about work-related transactions. Digital-age customer expectations are forcing companies to accelerate their digital transformation. Without the help of the performance evaluation community, companies won't be able to select the right applications and deployment models. As a result, companies risk losing time, money, and relevance in the eyes of their customers. Today, companies use the old standards of performance benchmarks to select technologies and infrastructure. In the future, they will need end-to-end performance evaluation for digital transformation workloads in order to accelerate their transformation. Performance evaluation complexity is about to increase many fold due to the use of distributed computing and a number of new technologies in digital transformation. The performance evaluation community will have to invent new approaches to providing end-to-end performance measures for digital transformation workloads.

Keywords: Digital transformation · Performance evaluation

1 Evolution of Performance Evaluation

Over the last few decades, multiple waves of new technologies drove the evolution of performance evaluation. These technologies and the applications incorporating them were initially run on servers dedicated to individual applications. The initial goal of performance evaluation was to provide a measure of performance for companies to choose technologies and applications running on dedicated servers. Each new generation of server CPUs provided improved performance using faster clock speeds, more memory support, more cores, and more hooks to improve application performance. The performance evaluation community also added new benchmarks as new technologies came to market [1]. Figure 1 shows the early evolution of performance benchmarking.

Eventually, IT infrastructure started moving from dedicated servers on-premise to virtualized servers on-premise. Performance benchmarking complexity began to increase over the years due to increasing levels of virtualization. With the advent of Infrastructure-as-a-Service (IaaS), companies started using virtualized servers running off-premise and this added additional complexity of performance evaluation. The next evolution of benchmarking had to handle the complexity of on/off-premise virtualized and containerized application deployments. Benchmarking organizations started addressing the complexity associated with these changes with additional benchmarks that included the ability

R. Nambiar and M. Poess (Eds.): TPCTC 2020, LNCS 12752, pp. 48–57, 2021.
https://doi.org/10.1007/978-3-030-84924-5_4

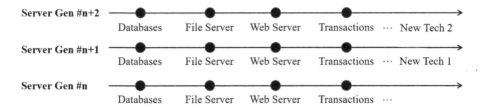

Performance Benchmarks

Fig. 1. Early evolution of performance evaluation

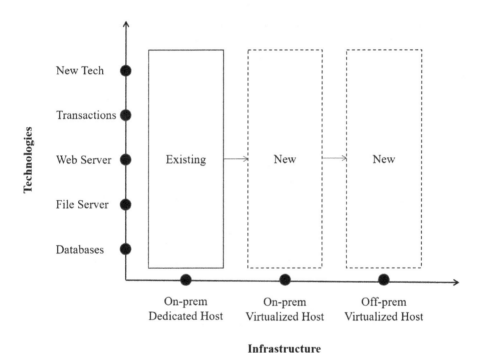

Infrastructure

Fig. 2. Performance evaluation complexity with new infrastructure models

to understand the implications of virtualization on-premise and off-premise. Figure 2 shows the increasing complexity of performance evaluation.

Transaction Processing Performance Council (TPC) has stayed relevant as new infrastructures and technologies appeared in the evaluation landscape [2]. But the accelerating pace of digital transformation will bring more challenges to performance benchmarking. The underlying cause for the explosion of the use of these new technologies are the digital-age customers.

2   Customer Expectations in the Digital Age

Customers value many things over and above product features and their consumer experiences blend into their B2B interactions. This means they expect consumer-like conveniences when dealing with companies in their work environment. Companies that meet these expectations will be more valuable to digital-age customers. Typical expectations customers have when they do business with a company are [3]:

- Mobile: Mobile interactions are the most common way for consumers to deal with businesses, and this trend continues to grow stronger. Customers do everything while they are on the move. They pull out cell phones to check stock prices, order online, track a package, pay for things, and watch a how-to video.
- Everything as a Service: For a while, ownership was the only way to get access to certain things, so customers went along with the only option and bought items to get access to them. In the digital age, customers own only the things that they want to possess or those that do not make financial sense to get as a service.
- Search: Customers start their journey with a search for products that help them do what they need to do. If a company does not show up in search results, it might as well not exist.
- Personalized: Customers want almost everything personalized. They don't buy bundles of products; they want to acquire precisely the part of the package they want.
- Secure: Customers want companies to protect the data they collect about them. They also require the connected products they buy to be secure. Customers want every financial transaction they make encrypted and not hackable. They also don't want companies to collect information from personal devices without their knowledge.
- Fast: Customers want instant gratification. How about two-hour delivery? They want to visualize how a paint color will look on our bedroom wall. Customers want to see how a piece of clothing will look on them without going to a store.
- Free: Customers want things to be free to use. They will trade privacy for free stuff. They will listen/view advertisements to get something for free.
- Cheap: If customers cannot get something for free, they want it to be as inexpensive as possible. They buy only after price comparisons.
- Social: Customers check online reviews before purchasing everything. They post reviews about their good and bad experiences. Customers look at items others purchased with the things they buy. They check Pinterest and Instagram for how other people use products they are considering. Social interaction is so prevalent that customers get suspicious if they cannot interact with a company.
- Transparency: Customers want companies to provide transparency on environmental and supply chain activities. They have started to consider how company operations impact the environment and want companies not to use child or bonded labor, poor working conditions, conflict minerals, or unfair trade practices.

3   Acceleration of Digital Transformation

The technologies we have available today are potent enablers for competitors within an industry and potential industry disrupters. Competitors wield digital technologies to attack profit pools and provide more value to customers by offering:

- Products that are better than their competitors'
- Lower cost of ownership for their products
- Consumer-like experiences in the B2B customer journey.

Company business strategies decay every day, and what was once a great business strategy may not be so great now. In the digital age, this rate of decay has accelerated because of:

- Changing customer expectations
- Technological advances
- Investment in new entrants who disrupt industries
- Huge, tech-savvy companies can get into industries with ease.

To stay relevant and profitable today, companies must offer more value to their customers than others. Product capabilities and cost of ownership are essential components of the value to the customer. But to thrive in the digital age, B2B businesses must understand the extras that digital-age customers value.

Given the pace of change in the business world, if companies don't update their business strategy and business model for the digital age, they will become irrelevant to customers. It is relatively easy to deal with incremental product and cost improvements provided by a competitor, but a significantly better, cheaper, or an easy to use competitive product will force companies to change how they operate their business. It is important to note that in the digital age, value to the customer, not technology, will force companies to change how they operate [3].

4   The Digital Transformation Stack

Changing old ways of doing business to meet digital-age customer expectations is the essence of digital transformation. Therefore, digital transformation requires changes to business processes. The business process stack comprises of:

1. Business applications
2. Technologies
3. Data
4. Infrastructure

Figure 3 shows a high-level view of the digital transformation stack with some of the new technologies and infrastructure choices. Although cybersecurity is not the focus of this paper, security is an overarching requirement in the digital age. With digital operations, companies collect data at all touchpoints with customers, suppliers, and employees. In addition they generate a large quantity of data from their products and business processes. This data must be protected using encryption and by securing the applications and infrastructure.

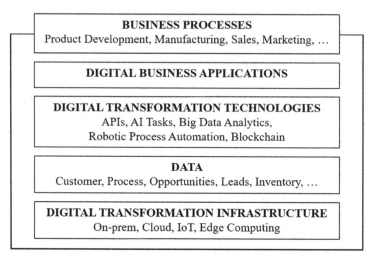

Fig. 3. The digital transformation stack

The high-level components of the business process stack are the same before and after digital transformation. However, the new technology and infrastructure choices used in the transformation are where the performance evaluation complexity increases. Data is a key component of digital transformation, but in this paper, we will focus on the infrastructure and technologies, because, these are areas where companies can make bad choices.

5   Digital Transformation Infrastructure

Performance evaluation organizations have made good progress in establishing benchmarks for IoT [4], but the rest of the infrastructure used for digital transformation has had limited focus from the performance evaluation community.

5.1   Cloud

Cloud means a lot of things to a lot of people. For our purpose, we will narrow the definition of Cloud to IaaS. IaaS allows companies to rent computing and storage capacity on-demand from a service provider. Companies can rent a whole device or part of a device and run their business apps on the rented devices. The service provider owns the rented devices and will operate the machines. Customers usually do performance evaluations on their own or engage consultants to do competitive benchmarking. This situation is not going to change for a while because customers typically need to evaluate the performance of their specific workloads before migrating them from their data center to the Cloud.

5.2 Internet of Things (IoT)

Tens of billions of devices will connect to the internet in the next few years. The term IoT describes the use of devices (things with sensors and actuators) sending data to a data store over the network, followed by a person or automated process controlling the device over a network. Three aspects of IoT that need special attention from a performance evaluation point of view are:

1. The device that collects information: The data collected can be anything that the device can sense within itself or in its surroundings. Customers can collect any data they think will create value to the customer or their own business. What are the evaluation criteria for IoT devices?
2. The connection (network and protocols) used to transmit the data collected by the IoT device: This connection plays a big part in the performance of the overall IoT implementation. Can the connection scale to a large number of IoT devices? Can the connection provide the required response times at scale?
3. The process that triggers an action based on the device data: An automated process can be used to analyze the device data and take action. For example, if a vending machine reports that it has only three bottles of water left, an automated process can schedule someone to replenish water. If the vending machine says the temperature inside is not cold enough to chill water, the automated process can schedule a maintenance event. The vending machine example may not convey the scaling challenges of process automation. Can the process scale to thousands of IoT devices? Can the process provide the required response times at scale?

5.3 Edge Computing

There is no standard definition for edge computing, but it is getting a lot of attention and is often pulled into digital transformation marketing, adding to the confusion around a lack of definition. In its simplest definition, edge computing brings computation closer to where the data originates or gets used. Today the typical edge computing use cases are in IoT implementation, but edge computing is useful in non-IoT use cases such as content distribution networks as well. Four factors decide whether data should be processed close to the source of the data.

1. Time value: If the data is not analyzed or accessed fast, it becomes useless
2. Communication cost: If the volume of data is large and it will cost a lot to send it to and retrieve it from the Cloud
3. Data privacy and security: If protected private information must be stored within the required geography
4. Service reliability: If distributing functionality among many redundant edge devices results in better service reliability.

Edge computing deserves special attention from the performance evaluation community due to the number of new technologies and applications under consideration for edge deployment.

6 Digital Transformation Technologies

Basic technologies like web front-end, mobile apps, e-commerce engines, digital maps, and weather maps are very important in the digital age. However, for the purposes of this paper, we will focus on technologies making their way from consumer interactions to the B2B world. Some of these technologies stayed as niche research topics for decades and became mainstream only after plenty of cheap computing became available. Performance benchmarking for Big Data Analytics is available now [5], and TPC has established a working group to address the performance evaluation of AI tasks [6]. More work remains in developing performance benchmarks for these technologies.

6.1 B2B APIs

Business to Business Application Programming Interfaces (B2B APIs) allow businesses to transfer information between their computers. Social media companies, supply chain companies, language translation services, and image recognition services all provide B2B APIs. APIs help automate internal processes as well as interactions with customers and partners. Automated tasks will, of course, increase agility and decrease cost for companies, their customers, and their partners.

6.2 AI Tasks

AI tasks like machine learning, inference engines, natural language processing, and machine vision allow computers to figure out their environment and achieve predefined goals.

Machine Learning is an AI task where computers develop a mathematical model from lots of input data. machine learning uses many algorithms, including some that mimic functions of neurons found in our brains. The vital factor is to understand that the "learned" mathematical model is only as good as the data used for learning. machines learn from past data, and there will be historical biases in the data. Biased data will result in biased mathematical models, and biased models will result in discriminatory predictions and decisions.

Inference and Recommendation Engines. Inference engines use mathematical models developed using machine learning to make predictions or decisions. Inference engines were part of the expert systems craze in the 1980s. expert systems have two components, a knowledge base, and an inference engine. The knowledgebase contains rules to handle specific situations and tasks from human experts. A simple inference engine could then detect the case and apply the rules provided by the experts. An expert system is usually the basis for many of the chatbots. Machine learning generated mathematical models augment the knowledgebase in newer chatbots.

A recommendation engine is a specialized inference engine that makes recommendations based on past activities and trends. These specialized engines are behind the recommended products when customers shop online.

Machine Vision is the AI task used to make a computer see what is in its environment. optical and thermal sensors are the starting point for machine vision. Image processing algorithms clean up the image provided by the sensor. From these images, one can detect text, check dimensions, recognize people and things, etc., using image detection algorithms. business processes use machine vision paired with inference engines and expert systems. A typical use case is detecting defects in manufacturing plants. Inference engines use mathematical models generated by machine learning and biased data can lead to erroneous inference, especially in facial recognition.

Natural Language Processing is the AI task used to make a computer understand human language and respond using human language. input to and outputs from NLP systems can be text (in data files or images provided by a sensor) or sound. A variety of algorithms that detect key concepts, themes, topics, contexts, and sentiments are the basis of NLP. The use of machine learning allowed NLP technologies to improve their accuracy in the last decade. Companies can detect trends (from customer issues, twitter feed, etc.) or create chatbots (text and audio) using an NLP system along with an Inference Engine.

6.3 Robotic Process Automation

Robotics involves building machines that can execute tasks specified by a computer program. Robots are designed using AI tasks mentioned above, along with electronic and mechanical components. Robots can automate processes that are (a) repetitive or (b) threaten human health. Robotic process automation (RPA) lowers cost by reducing labor costs and improves quality by reducing human error.

The word robot brings up images of human-looking androids and robotic car manufacturing lines. However, if we use the definition "machine that can do a task specified by a computer program," we can build robots without mechanical elements, so RPA now includes software only robots that automate tasks linking many business applications. For example, a customer's email requesting service can automatically file a service ticket, order replacement parts, and invite the customer to schedule service. Software-only RPA provides better agility and responsiveness on top of cost reduction and higher accuracy.

6.4 Big Data Analytics

Business analytics to derive insights from data for improving business performance has been around for decades. Companies now collect a large amount of data from every customer interaction, every employee interaction, and every machine to machine interaction. Analyzing this extensive collection of data (big data) needs special techniques collectively called Big Data Analytics.

6.5 Blockchain

Blockchain allows companies in a network to record secure transactions in a shared ledger. The shared ledger builds trust about the transaction without requiring an intermediary. Removing trusted intermediaries from transactions allow efficient and less expensive transactions. Today, operations like traceable sourcing, insurance, and many others use blockchain. Blockchain transactions will appear more and more in many industries.

7 Performance Evaluation to Support Digital Transformation

The diversity of the new technologies and the distributed computing introduced by the emerging infrastructure adds another dimension to performance evaluation. Figure 4 shows the next stage in the evolution of performance evaluation.

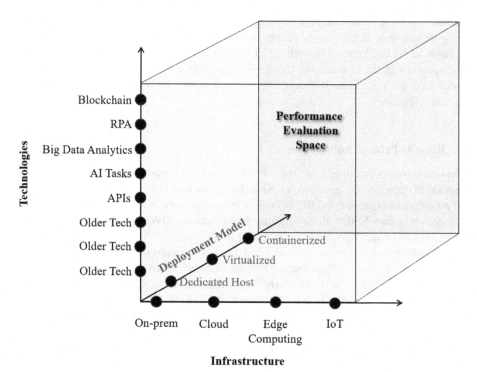

Fig. 4. Complexity in evaluating performance for digital transformation

Additional complexity is introduced to performance evaluation in the digital transformation era because companies do not buy every component of the stack from a single vendor. Traversing the large space in the three-dimensional map shown in Fig. 4 now requires performance evaluation at each handoff point between the technologies and the components of the infrastructure. Also, companies are not just looking for raw performance of the elements in their stack. They need to assess how a transformed process addresses the expectations of digital-age customers.

Performance evaluation and benchmarking have allowed companies to select technologies, applications, and infrastructure over the past few decades. As companies go through digital transformation, they will need end-to-end performance evaluations for their newly transformed business processes. The diversity of applications and technologies, along with distributed computing purchased from multiple vendors, will require the performance evaluation community to develop new approaches to benchmark evolving digital transformation use cases.

References

1. SPEC.org Homepage. https://www.spec.org/benchmarks.html. Accessed 08 Aug 2020
2. Nambiar, R., Poess, M.: Keeping the TPC relevant! Proc. VLDB Endow. **6**, 1186–1187 (2013)
3. Gopalakrishnan, S.: Purposeful Digital Transformation, 1st edn. California (2020)
4. Poess, M., et al.: Analysis of TPCx-IoT: the first industry standard benchmark for IoT gateway systems. In: IEEE 34th International Conference on Data Engineering, pp. 1519–1530 (2018)
5. Han, R., John, L., Zhan, J.: Benchmarking big data systems: a review. IEEE Trans. Serv. Comput. **11**(3), 580–597 (2017)
6. Nambiar, R., Poess, M. (eds.): TPCTC 2018. LNCS, vol. 11135. Springer, Cham (2019). https://doi.org/10.1007/978-3-030-11404-6

Experimental Comparison of Relational and NoSQL Document Systems: The Case of Decision Support

Tomás F. Llano-Ríos[1](✉) [iD], Mohamed Khalefa[2], and Antonio Badia[1]

[1] University of Louisville, Louisville, KY 40208, USA
{tfllan01,abadia}@louisville.edu
[2] SUNY College Old Westbury, Old Westbury, NY 11568, USA
khalefam@oldwestbury.edu

Abstract. We design and implement an experimental analysis comparing a relational system (PostgreSQL) and two document-based NoSQL systems (MongoDB and Couchbase) on a single server, Decision Support (DSS) scenario. We argue that DSS is becoming an important case study for NoSQL. We experiment with several database designs and several query formulations in order to investigate the effect of physical design and query optimization in document-based stores. Our results show that design is very important for document stores performance, and that query optimization over documents is less sophisticated than in relational systems and needs to improve. Our results offer some guidance in this area.

1 Introduction

In some environments, NoSQL systems can be considered as an alternative to relational database systems (RDBMS) for certain kinds of problems [2]. This leads to a need for comparisons, even though comparing NoSQL systems with traditional relational databases is difficult due to differences in data models and query languages.

In this paper, we compare experimentally a relational system (PostgreSQL) and two document-oriented NoSQL systems (MongoDB and Couchbase). We focus our comparison on Decision Support (DSS) tasks (answering complex queries over static data), and we limit our comparison to a single-node setting to compare the 'pure' performance of each system and its optimizer capabilities. While not an environment that fits most NoSQL systems, we argue that it is an important test, for several reasons. First, as analysis goes to where the data is, NoSQL systems will likely be used for DSS as they gain a bigger foothold—in fact, MongoDB has recently expanded the capabilities of its query language (e.g., the $lookup operator, a new aggregating pipeline), a strong indicator that customers demand the ability to write more complex queries. Second, even if NoSQL systems are mostly deployed in distributed settings, performance within a node is still very important [4]. Finally, as NoSQL systems are still relatively

© Springer Nature Switzerland AG 2021
R. Nambiar and M. Poess (Eds.): TPCTC 2020, LNCS 12752, pp. 58–74, 2021.
https://doi.org/10.1007/978-3-030-84924-5_5

new and evolving, this is a good moment to analyze weaknesses and strengths to guide further developments.

We focus on the document data model since it is close to nested relations ([1]), making comparison with relational a bit easier. We use MongoDB and Couchbase as representatives of document-based systems. Mongodb uses a proprietary, *navigational* query language, one which is part declarative and part procedural. Couchbase, on the other hand, uses an SQL-like language. Unlike past work that has compared NoSQL and relational systems [2,3,5] we focus on DSS and examine in depth MongoDB's and Couchbase's query language and data model and their influence on performance. As a result, our efforts are complementary to those of [2,3,5]. We argue that some of the lessons learned in our experiments extend to other document-based systems.

We base our experimental analysis on the TPC-H benchmark [6], as it is a well-known, established DSS benchmark. In order not to put document-based systems at a disadvantage, we limit ourselves to data that can be nicely represented within a document data model (basically, we eliminate many-to-many relations; see Sect. 2 for details). We analyze the results paying special attention to MongoDB's and Couchbase's query optimizer behavior.

The main contributions of the paper are: (1) We design an experiment comparing PostgreSQL and two document-based NoSQL systems on a DSS workload. (2) We perform additional, tailored experiments (denoted as *micro-benchmarks*) to study the influence of factors like database design, presence/absence of indices, and order of operators in query performance, and (3) We provide a thorough analysis to evaluate the strengths and limitations of document stores for DSS.

Due to lack of space, we assume the reader is familiar with the required background (the document data model, and MongoDB's query language). We also skip an in-depth comparison with related work; as stated above, our efforts are complementary to existing ones. All data, queries, and code used are available at https://github.com/tllano11/dss-sql-vs-nosql-experiments. Interested readers can contact the first author for any further information.

2 Experiments

All experiments are run on an IBM System x3650 M2 server with two Intel Xeon X5672 processors at 3.20 GHz, 16 virtual cores, and 46 GB of RAM. The server runs CentOS Linux version 7.6.1810, MongoDB version 4.0.6, Couchbase version 6.5, and PostgreSQL version 10.6. The operating system and both databases are tuned according to best practices. All queries are run five times and the average running time is reported. After every single execution, the cache of the operating system and both databases is cleared.

2.1 Data

We use the TPC-H dataset at five scale factors (1G, 10G, 25G, 50G, 100G); where the last two sizes do not fit in memory. The data was generated using the TPC-H benchmark's generation tool (DBGEN) [6]. We only consider one-to-many relationships for data modeling, thus only TPC-H tables Customer, Orders and Lineitem are used (called C, O and L, respectively, in this experiment). We store the data in PostgreSQL in plain relational following the TPC-H schema and create an extra table (called $\mathcal{JCOL}$) using the JSONB datatype to store the content of C, O and L as embedded records. In MongoDB and Couchbase we model the one-to-many relationship through the schemas below:

- **Denormalized schema (S.1):** Customers (from C) have an array with 0 or more orders (from O) and these, in turn, an array of lineitems (from L). We use a single collection in MongoDB and a single bucket in Couchbase–named $\mathcal{MCOL}$ and $\mathcal{CBCOL}$ respectively–to implement this schema.
- **Normalized schema (S.2):** Documents reside in collections ($\mathcal{MC}$, $\mathcal{MO}$, and $\mathcal{ML}$) and buckets ($\mathcal{CBC}$, $\mathcal{CBO}$, and $\mathcal{CBL}$) in MongoDB and Couchbase respectively. Linking is represented by attributes o_custkey in $\mathcal{MO}$ and $\mathcal{CBO}$, referencing a customer, and l_orderkey in $\mathcal{ML}$ and $\mathcal{CBL}$, referencing an order.
- **Hybrid schema (S.3):** Document reside in collections $\mathcal{MC}$ and $\mathcal{MOL}$ in MongoDB and buckets $\mathcal{CBC}$ and $\mathcal{CBOL}$ in Couchbase. $\mathcal{MC}$ and CBC are the same as in S.2. The other two embed lineitems into orders and use a link to reference customers. Linking is represented by the attribute o_custkey. This approach is symmetrical to embedding orders into customers and creating a link from lineitems to orders as each one favors certain queries at the expense of others. Therefore, looking at one in terms of performance gives us insight into the other.

2.2 Queries

We only use tables C, O and L, thus we restrict our attention to the TPC-H queries queries Q1, Q3, Q4, Q12, Q13 and Q22. Their parameters are modified to increase selectivity and help us analyze index performance. We create a micro-benchmark with ad-hoc queries to investigate several issues noted during experimentation. These are discussed in Sect. 2.3.

For each TPC-H query we create two PostgreSQL queries, one using SQL as a foundation and one querying $\mathcal{JCOL}$ (we refer to these queries as "JSONB queries" for simplicity). To investigate the impact of using different operators we write each query for the document stores in different ways, called versions.

MongoDB and Couchbase's optimizers generate query plans that follow the query as is, with only a minor reordering of some operations. We explore different combinations of operators in MongoDB and Couchbase to evaluate the influence in their ordering within a query. We remark that correlated sub-queries are often difficult (sometimes impossible) to do in Couchbase without expressing the correlation as a join. Couchbase recommends having a single bucket with multiple data groups, where each one is identified by selections over a <type> attribute, but this introduces ambiguity because every join is a self-join.

To differentiate between versions we use the following naming conventions: For PostgreSQL, q<num>_psql and q<num>_psql_json, where <num> is a TPC-H query number and `json` means the query uses the JSONB data type. For the document stores, `q<num>[v<ver>]_<engine>_<schema>`, where `<num>` is the corresponding TPC-H query number, `<ver>` the version number, `<engine>` equal to "cb" for Couchbase and "mongo" for MongoDB, and `<schema>` refers to queries running on S.1, S.2, or S.3. MongoDB versions are explained in Table 1 and serve the purpose of: (1) Showing what filtering method performs better on arrays. The combination of operators `$unwind` and `$match`; or `$project`, `$filter` and `$unwind`. Query versions 1 and 2 on S.1 help to clarify this by filtering nested documents using these combinations. (2) Determining multi-key indexes reliability on documents nested more than one level as not much is known of their performance on such scenarios. Query version 3 on S.1 helps us validate this. (3) Determining if "direction" of a join influences running time. In MongoDB's aggregation framework design the starting collection of a pipeline defines the direction of a join and reversing the direction implies re-creating the entire query. Query versions 1, 2, 3 on S.2 and 1, 2 on S.3 help to measure the impact of joining from different directions.

Table 1. Description of version number according to the schema

Schema	Version	Meaning
S.1	1	Use $filter to filter objects within an array and $unwind to retrieve elements from within it
S.1	2	Use $unwind to retrieve elements from within an array and $match to filter them
S.1	3	Use an extra $match meant to trigger MongoDB's optimizer to use an index, if any
S.2	1	Start pipeline at $\mathcal{MO}$, lookup from $\mathcal{ML}$, and $\mathcal{MC}$ thereafter
S.2	2	Start pipeline at $\mathcal{MC}$, lookup from $\mathcal{MO}$, and $\mathcal{ML}$ thereafter
S.2	3	Start pipeline at $\mathcal{ML}$, lookup from $\mathcal{MO}$, and $\mathcal{MC}$ thereafter
S.3	1	Start pipeline at $\mathcal{MOL}$ and lookup from $\mathcal{MC}$
S.3	2	Start pipeline at $\mathcal{MC}$ and lookup from $\mathcal{MOL}$

Couchbase has well documented limitations like the lack of join reordering[1] and a cost-based optimizer (they recently added a cost-based optimizer on the enterprise edition of version 6.5[2]). Couchbase's query versions (explained in Table 2) don't address these, but other non-documented difficulties at reordering query predicates to increase performance: *Selection push-down within join predicate*–tested on query 3; this query does not have sub-queries, performs simple aggregations, selects elements from and joins the three tables $\mathcal{C}$, $\mathcal{O}$, and $\mathcal{L}$, and its major bottleneck resides in the join. If an optimizer does not push-down

---

[1] https://blog.couchbase.com/why-cost-based-optimizer-for-nosql-n1ql-couchbase/.
[2] https://blog.couchbase.com/cost-based-optimizer-for-couchbase-n1ql-sql-for-json/.

Table 2. Description of version number for Couchbase queries according to the schema

Schema	Query	Version	Meaning
S.2	3	1	No explicit selection push-down on $\mathcal{CBC}$
S.2	3	2	Explicit selection push-down on $\mathcal{CBC}$
S.1	13	1	Filter orders using LEFT OUTER UNNEST and WHERE
S.1	13	2	Filter orders using the ARRAY operator
S.1	13	3	Explicit projection of orders after LEFT OUTER UNNEST and later filter using WHERE
S.2/S.3	22	1	Compute customers without orders using an uncorrelated sub-query, store result set LET and match in WHERE using IN
S.2/S.3	22	2	Compute customers without orders in the WHERE using an uncorrelated sub-query and match using IN
S.2/S.3	22	3	Similar to version 2, but the average account balances are saved using LET prior to the WHERE clause and the selection over c_phone is included when computing the set of customers without orders
S.2/S.3	22	4	Filter $\mathcal{CBC}$ based on c_phone predicate, then left join with $\mathcal{CBO}$ and select customers without orders. Here, the combination of the uncorrelated sub-query and IN operator present in previous versions is replaced by the left join and further selection described earlier

the selections on the WHERE clause of this query, the database would scan all tables without selecting subsets of each beforehand. We create a version where selections are pushed-down and one where they are not to verify if Couchbase applies the optimization. *Filtering in nested structures*, tested on query 13; this query only evaluates conditions on $\mathcal{O}$ and its bottleneck in S.1 depends on the c_orders array only. Like MongoDB, Couchbase offers different alternatives to evaluate conditions in the structure: Flattening the array using UNNEST and filter using WHERE or looping through the array and filter using ARRAY. Versions 1 and 2, respectively, test these combinations. Version 3 tests if unnesting c_orders within a sub-query, then projecting and filtering using WHERE improves performance over version 1. *Correlated sub-query*, tested on query 22. Correlated sub-queries cannot be written in Couchbase's N1QL query language when they refer to documents from a different bucket, so they must be rewritten as a join (semi-join in query 4's case) or using IN and an uncorrelated sub-query. Versions 1 through 4 test the performance of expressing the correlated sub-query through different combinations of operators.

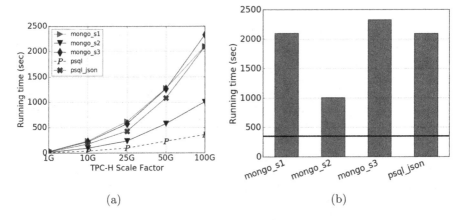

Fig. 1. Running times of Q1 on MongoDB and PostgreSQL

2.3   Results

The graphs in Figs. 1, 4, 7, 9, 11, and 12 show the running times of MongoDB, PostgreSQL relational and JSONB query versions. Each figure shows one TPC-H query at the 5 tested scale factors. There are two graphs per query: a line chart where the x-axis displays all five scale factors while the y-axis displays the running time of each implementation for a given scale factor; and a bar chart showing the running times of all query versions at the 100G scale factor with one bar per version except for the relational SQL version

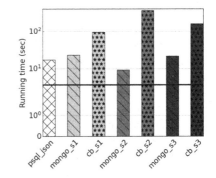

Fig. 2. Running time (in log scale) of Q1 on all databases using scale factor of 1G

(used as a baseline), which is denoted by the black line. Note that the bar chart focuses on the rightmost point of the line chart to show in more detail what happens at the largest scale (in the line charts, some lines are very close because some versions were much slower than others; hence they must show a wide range).

We tested Couchbase versions at the 1G scale factor only because of their poor performance. The results we report for them are the best obtained after extensive manual query rewriting. Charts in Figs. 2, 3, 5, 6, 8, 10 compare their running times with the other databases. The relational SQL version of each query is used as a baseline and is represented by the horizontal black line parallel to the x-axis. The white bar represents the PostgreSQL JSONB version of a query, bars with the same gray tone indicate versions in the same schema (S.1, S.2, S.3), and bars with the same hatch indicate versions in the same database (star for Couchbase, inverted diagonal line for MongoDB, crossed diagonals for PostgreSQL). The y-axis is shown in log scale to better display the results as run times were several orders of magnitude higher in Couchbase than MongoDB and Post-greSQL. During experimentation we set a time limit of 24 h; queries exceeding it are killed and their running time not measured. Versions on schemas S.2 and S.3 on MongoDB tend to exceed the limit in queries that use the $lookup operator, thus we create indexes on o_custkey (for $\mathcal{MO}$ and $\mathcal{MOL}$), and l_orderkey (for $\mathcal{ML}$) to help this operator perform better—all collections have an index on the _id field, created by default). Even though this decreases running times somewhat, some of them are still killed. Additionally, we create indexes on foreign keys in PostgreSQL and linking attributes in Couchbase to make a fair comparison. We refer to this strategy as *key-only indexes*; alternatives that use additional indices are explored in Subsect. 2.3.

We present a summary of the results obtained per query below. From this section onward we define a query q to be *fitting* a data group (collection or bucket) G to indicate that all attributes mentioned in q are part of the objects in a MongoDB collection or Couchbase bucket G so that q can be run on G alone. The description of each query refers to the original (SQL) formulation. The observed results for queries can be summarized as follow:

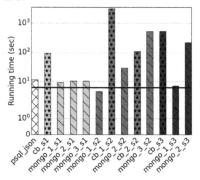

Fig. 3. Running time (in log scale) of Q3 on all databases using scale factor of 1G

Query 1 Because the query only requires attributes from $\mathcal{L}$, our initial hypothesis is that versions on S.1 and S.3 are at a disadvantage since, in both cases, the documents of interest (lineitems) are stored inside arrays as nested objects, thus making necessary to use extra operators for their retrieval. In MongoDB these would be $project (with $filter) or $unwind followed by $match. In Couchbase this would be UNNEST. Queries run on S.2 scan smaller documents

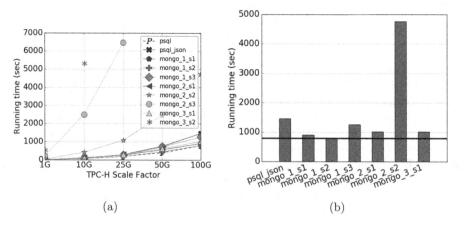

(a)   (b)

Fig. 4. Running times of Q3 on MongoDB and PostgreSQL

and do not require these extra stages; which explains why they are faster in MongoDB (Nonetheless, q1_mongo_s2 is more than 50% slower than q1_psql). This can also be observed with JSONB due to heavy unnesting.

In Couchbase, Fig. 2 shows this hypothesis does not hold. Depending on storage details, scanning more documents can be more costly; especially if all or most of them are fetched from disk. This, plus the UNNEST operator happening in-memory–therefore not adding much to the cost–may explain why Couchbase version on S.2 is slower than on S.3, and the version on S.3 slower than on S.1.

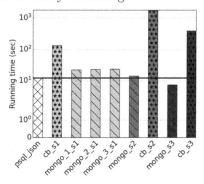

Fig. 5. Running time (in log scale) of Q4 on all databases using scale factor of 1G

Query 3 Schema S.2 can result in either the best or worst running times; query plan analysis reveals the reason. Versions 2 and 3 on MongoDB perform very poorly, with the latter not even finishing on the 25G scale factor. On these versions, joins translate into two lookups; the first one scans $\mathcal{MO}$, and the second one $\mathcal{ML}$ and $\mathcal{MC}$ respectively. Version 1 lookups from $\mathcal{MC}$ first and $\mathcal{ML}$ second. Because $\mathcal{MO}$ is approximately 82.55% larger than $\mathcal{MC}$ its scanning takes considerably more time, thus versions 2 and 3 spend more time in the first lookup than version 1. Results show that the first lookup is, in fact, a bottleneck on query 3 when it scans any MongoDB

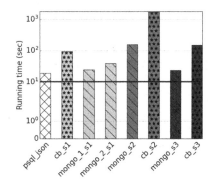

Fig. 6. Running time (in log scale) of Q12 on all databases using scale factor of 1G

equivalent of $\mathcal{O}$, as the same behavior is present in query q3v2_mongo_s3. Because lineitems are embedded into orders in $\mathcal{MOL}$, a second lookup in this query is not needed and running time decreases compared to version 3 on S.2; but on q3v1_mongo_s3 it can be seen (again) that scanning $\mathcal{MC}$ is cheaper. we believe q3v1_mongo_s2 is faster than q3v1_mongo_s3 because the cost of joining $\mathcal{MOL}$ with $\mathcal{MC}$ is much higher than joining $\mathcal{MO}$ with $\mathcal{MC}$, as the size of documents in $\mathcal{MOL}$ is significantly greater than in $\mathcal{MO}$. Likewise, this behavior appears to also apply to the $unwind operator on S.1.

The cost of unwinding documents with big nested documents is bigger than joining two collections with smaller documents. In short, q3v1_mongo_s2 is the fastest query 3's MongoDB version because of the order in which collections are joined and the document size of each one. In Couchbase, Fig. 3 shows version 1 on S.2 is slower than on S.3 and S.1. This is because the system fetches all documents in the respective buckets of each schema and, as it was noted for

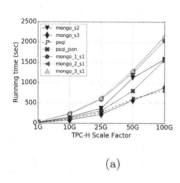
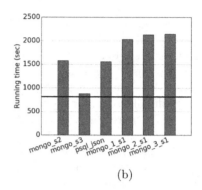

(a)   (b)

Fig. 7. Running times of Q4 on MongoDB and PostgreSQL

query 1, scanning more documents in Couchbase seems to have significantly more impact than the in-memory operators. Moreover, the system joins all documents before filtering, without pushing down any selection, which is highly detrimental for performance. For version 2 on S.2 we pushed down all selections explicitly, thus reducing the amount of documents to fetch and join. By doing so, running time decreased to be almost that of the version on S.1.

Query 4 A join is required in q4_mongo_s2 because the query does not fit $\mathcal{MO}$. Since it fits $\mathcal{MOL}$, q4_mongo_s3 benefits from this particular database design. The query also fits $\mathcal{MCOL}$, but queries on S.1 need to perform extra steps that seem to be particularly expensive: (1) use $unwind to deconstruct each array of orders per customer, and (2) use $group to re-group tuples of o_orderkey and o_oderpriority after unwinding o_lineitems. Specifically, by deconstructing o_lineitems new

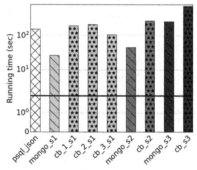

Fig. 8. Running time (in log scale) of Q13 on all databases using scale factor of 1G

documents are created per element in the array and each new document retains all other fields, thus tuples o_orderkey and o_orderpriority are not unique after such operation. The final result depends on the count of such unique tuples, thus they must be re-grouped. Couchbase favors S.1 given the smaller number of documents to scan. Just like in MongoDB the query fits $\mathcal{CBOL}$ and $\mathcal{CBCOL}$, but the former has an order of magnitude more documents. This makes q4_cb_s3 slower than q4_cb_s1. Given Couchbase's incomplete support for correlated sub-queries, q4_cb_s2 was modeled as a join between $\mathcal{CBO}$ and $\mathcal{CBL}$. The system scanned all buckets, joined them and filtered afterwards; which explains its poor performance.

Query 12 The MongoDB and Couchbase query versions on S.2 are significantly slower than the other versions. This is to be expected, as joining $\mathcal{MO}$ and $\mathcal{ML}$,

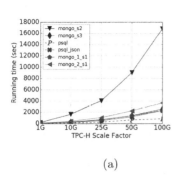

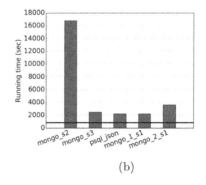

(a)   (b)

Fig. 9. Running times of Q12 on MongoDB and PostgreSQL

and $\mathcal{CBO}$ and $\mathcal{CBL}$ takes significant time given their sizes. For MongoDB queries on S.1 and S.3, the query fits $\mathcal{MCOL}$ and $\mathcal{MOL}$, respectively, but an extra unwind of the array of orders per customer is required for the former, which makes it slower than on the latter. Same logic applies to JSONB. In Couchbase, scanning $\mathcal{CBCOL}$ is cheaper than $\mathcal{CBOL}$, thus the query on S.1 is faster.

Query 13 Because of the left outer join, the MongoDB pipeline can only start from collection $\mathcal{MC}$ and lookup from $\mathcal{MO}$ in queries on S.2 and $\mathcal{MOL}$ on S.3.

As mentioned in Query 3, joining in this order leads to poor performance as scanning any MongoDB equivalent of $\mathcal{O}$ in $lookup is slower than scanning $\mathcal{MC}$. Figure 8 shows a similar behavior in Couchbase. Not surprisingly, versions on S.1 had lower running times as they fit

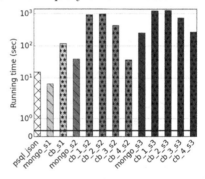

Fig. 10. Running time (in log scale) of Q22 on all databases using scale factor of 1G

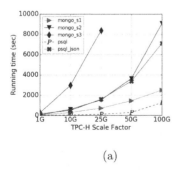

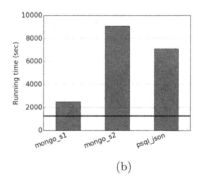

(a)   (b)

Fig. 11. Running times of Q13 on MongoDB and PostgreSQL

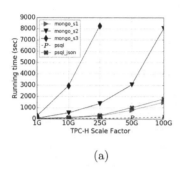
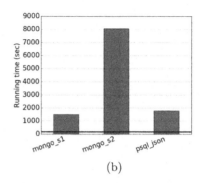

(a)   (b)

Fig. 12. Running times of Q22 on MongoDB and PostgreSQL

$\mathcal{JCOL}$, $\mathcal{ACOL}$, $\mathcal{MCOL}$ and $\mathcal{CBCOL}$, therefore, avoiding any $lookups in MongoDB and lest joins in Couchbase and PostgreSQL. Figure 8 also shows that filtering nested structures through unnest plus where is faster than using the array operator. Moreover, projecting specific fields from orders in q13v3_cb_s1 proved to be beneficial in decreasing running time for successive aggregation steps.

Query 22 Just like on Q1, queries over $\mathcal{JCOL}$ and $\mathcal{ACOL}$ are at a disadvantage compared to plain relational. All MongoDB queries must perform a self-join at a certain point in the pipeline, but after documents have passed by multiple stages the $lookup stage has to repeat the same steps leading to such point, which is highly inefficient. Specifically, by calculating the average account balance other fields (_id, c_acctbal, cntrycode) required later in the pipeline are lost due to the $group stage. Versions on S.2 and S.3 are the most affected by this because they need to go through $lookup before self-joining, which results in a nested $lookup stage. Given its poor performance, we write another version of the query using an alternative approach that could be more efficient. It consists of using the $addToSet operator instead of $lookup, in order to retain the fields that are originally lost.

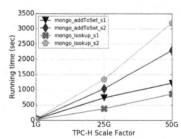

Fig. 13. Running times of Q22 on MongoDB using the $lookup stage or the $group stage + the $addToSet operator

Table 3. Description of point queries

Query id	Objective	What the query does
a	Evaluate the performance of $match plus $unwdind against $project and $filter plus $unwind	Select all lineitems where o_orderkey is equal to 7.
b	Evaluate how fast small and big documents are filtered	Select customer with c_custkey = 7 from $\mathcal{MC}$, and $\mathcal{MCOL}$.
c	Evaluate if the performance of joining a big collection with a small collection is affected by the direction of the join	Join pairs of collections in S.2: $\mathcal{MC} \wedge \mathcal{MO}$ (version 1), $\mathcal{MO} \wedge \mathcal{MC}$ (version 2), $\mathcal{MO} \wedge \mathcal{ML}$ (version 3), $\mathcal{ML} \wedge \mathcal{MO}$ (version 4).
d	Evaluate performance of coalescing an $unwind within a lookup and then filtering vs projecting a subset of the array created by $lookup and then using $unwind	Select customer id and order id for orders where o_totalprice ¿ 37500

On the queries run over schemas S.1 and S.2 we replace a $lookup stage meant to simulate a self-join with a combination of the $group stage and the $addToSet operator. Figure 13 shows the running time of these queries. The ones using $lookup have the *lookup* keyword in their name, while those using $group + $addToSet have *addToSet* in their names. The results show the use of $addToSet decreases running time on S.2 and S.3, but increases it on S.1—note that using the $push operator instead of $addToSet is also feasible; during experimentation we observed both approaches behave the same regarding $lookup. The bottleneck on the first two versions seems to be caused by the nested $lookup stage; by replacing it with $addToSet running time was decreased. On the third one, there is no nested $lookup stage, but filterings ($match) and a projection ($project). This appears to cost less than using the $addToSet operator. In Couchbase, the correlated sub-query within the *exists* operator had to be modeled as a join because of the system's limitations. Figure 10 shows that version 4 on S.2 is the fastest of all Couchbase queries. In that version, the selection over c_phone was included in the uncorrelated sub-query and the predicate filtering c_acctbal being greater than the average of positive account balances. Because all selections have been pushed-down in this version, it fetches less documents and is therefore faster.

In the majority of queries, except 3 and 4, the PostgreSQL (relational) implementation outperformed its MongoDB counterparts by more than 50% across scale factors. To help us explain this outcome we formulate a series of hypotheses below and test them using a self-created microbenchmark featuring the queries described in Table 3. We call these queries *point queries*:

- Query version 1 on S.1 is faster than version 2 for Q3, Q4 and Q12. We hypothesize it is faster to project a subset of an array based on a condition and then deconstruct it than first deconstruct it and then filter the result. We design point query a such that version 1 filters documents after unwinding field c_lineitems and version 2 projects a subset of the array before unwinding it. We use a value of o_orderkey for which less than 1% of $\mathcal{L}$ is retrieved. Figure 14a confirms our hypothesis as version 2 is faster than 1.
- Based on Q3's results we hypothesize retrieving big documents is slower than small ones. We test this with point query b by measuring the filtering speed of attributes at the top level of big and small documents. Figure 14b shows that scanning $\mathcal{MC}$ is faster than $\mathcal{MCOL}$. This validates the hypothesis, as the latter has documents with a much bigger size.

- On W3, a clear difference in running time can be noticed when comparing versions 1, 2 and 3 over S.3. We believe the order in which collections are joined greatly impacts performance. Specifically, we want to establish if the order of collections used to perform an equijoin (or equality match) by using $lookup has an actual effect on performance. We use point query c to test this. Figure 14c shows that starting the pipeline at $\mathcal{MO}$ is faster than at $\mathcal{MC}$ or $\mathcal{ML}$, We believe this is due to collection size, but our experiments cannot verify it. Nonetheless, we can confirm that the join's direction plays a crucial role in running time.
- Results from the TPC-H queries and point query a show that the combination $project, $filter and $unwind (approach 1) is faster than $unwind and $match (approach 2). When filtering elements of an array created by the $lookup stage both approaches perform the same because the optimizer coalesces $unwind (from approach 2) into $lookup. To verify this we create point query d. It tests both approaches after a $lookup. Figure 14d shows there is no major difference between them.

Indexes. To determine the impact of indexing, we add extra indices to the data. We identify attributes used in a selection in any query and, as a result, we create indices on l_shipdate, l_commitdate, l_receiptdate, o_orderdate, c_mktsegment, and c_acctbal. We call this strategy *extended indexing*. Note that the impact of indexes on the TPC-H Benchmark is very limited as many attributes have low cardinality and, thus, are not very selective.

We create extended indexes on the relational and JSONB queries, MongoDB and Couchbase queries on S.1 (typical schema on document stores). In MongoDB only the first stage and the $lookup stage can benefit from indexing because they ingest documents directly from a collection. Because of this limitation, most of these indexes cannot be effectively used on MongoDB; thus we only consider queries where one of them is used: queries 3 and 22.

We compare the selection of indexes each database makes below:
- For query 3 we use parameters [DATE]=1992-01-02, and [SEGMENT]='AUTOMOBILE'. The former is part of one condition involving o_orderdate and other involving l_shipdate. The first one selects 0.0414% of $\mathcal{O}$ and the second 99% of $\mathcal{L}$. The latter is part of a condition involving c_mktsegment and selects 19.83% of $\mathcal{C}$. Because MongoDB and JSONB queries used the index on c_mktsegment and PostgreSQL relational chose the one on o_orderdate, the results in Table 4 show PostgreSQL gets a better speed-up as data size increases and indicate that better selectivity leads to better performance. MongoDB uses an index whenever available, regardless of selectivity. This results in poor query plans. Indices in JSONB queries decrease performance. This is likely because PostgreSQL cannot collect statistics of the JSONB type unless a functional index is used. Couchbase scanned all three indexes, but only fetched documents matching the most selective predicate. This technique (called inter-sect scan[3]) achieved a significant speed-up by avoiding excessive hits to disk.

- For query 22, the only possible index selection is the one on c_acctbal. There are two conditions related to such attribute: One matching positive account balances–selecting ∼90% of $\mathcal{C}$–and another matching account balances greater than the average of positive account balances–selecting ∼45% of $\mathcal{C}$.

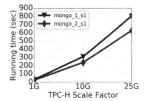

(a) Point query a

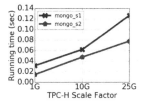

(b) Point query b

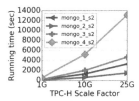

(c) Point query c

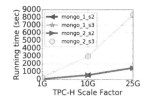

(d) Point query d

Fig. 14. Running times of queries in the microbenchmark

---

[3] https://dzone.com/articles/performance-ingredients-for-nosql-intersect-scans.

Table 4. Speedup gained by using indexes. Negative percentages mean using indexes made the implementation slower

Query	SF: 1G	SF: 10G	SF: 25G
q3_psql	1.60%	26.71%	27.95%
q3_psql_json	0.78%	−11.15%	−6.05%
q3v1_mongo_s1	4.93%	9.16%	9.37%
q3v2_mongo_s1	2.43%	9.29%	9.62%
q3v3_mongo_s1	4.55%	10.41%	9.61%
q22_mongo_s1	−2944.67%	−2291.34%	−1992.62%
q22_psql	−1.66%	7.50%	1.27%
q22_psql_json	0.62%	23.69%	24.12%

All PostgreSQL queries use the index on the second condition, while the Mon-goDB version uses it on the first one; which has a detrimental impact on performance as shown in Table 4. Results confirm that MongoDB uses an index without considering the selectivity factor.

2.4   Analysis and Discussion

Our experimental results support the following points:

· An arbitrary query q will not always be faster over a single collection than several. In our experiment, no query over S.1 requires joins, while queries over S.2 and S.3 may require them. Queries over S.1 are not always faster because they scan more data. Also, q may require a selection deep into a complex document structure. This involves a costly array deconstruction. There exists a clear trade-off between designing the database with one (or a few) complex, deeply nested objects, and several, but smaller, data units confirmed by our experiments: if q fits in a collection in S.2 or S.3, then q will run slower in S.1. This can be seen, for instance, in query 1 where versions on S.2 were 50% faster (across scales) than those on S.1. This is expected as q scans fewer data in S.2. If q uses unnest to retrieve fields from the deepest object/s of documents in S.1, q would be faster in S.2 or S.3. Results of query 4 show this: using S.2 decreased running time by up to 22.4% and S.3 by up to 56% (both on the 100GB scale). Since Couchbase's bottleneck resides on document fetching, something that can be seen in all Couchbase queries without manual optimization (pattern of S.1 faster than S.3, faster than S.2), using in-memory operators like UNNEST is preferred as nested structures speed up performance by minimizing fetching.

· In a pure relational approach the order of selections depends on that of joins. In the 'document' side, it depends on the structure of the document. One can force selections to go 'top to bottom' in the structure of the data, which does not seem to harm performance, but the query must be manually optimized.

Depending on the database's workload one must choose between using nesting (embedding) or linking. Simpler objects in several collections favor queries that are covered by a single one, but do not perform well when joins are required; complex objects in a single collection do not need joins but suffer when only parts of the object (especially nested parts) are involved. In any case, schema design is important for performance.

· If a database is designed using several collections, join-like operations must be supported. This has the advantage that it allows a document-based database to deal with many-to-many relationships without undue duplication, but brings in the complexities of efficiently supporting such an operator. Unlike relational databases, joins in document stores have several limitations and sometimes bugs[4]). One must consider this before choosing a schema. In a navigational language, it is likely that the order of joins is determined by how the query is written because it is expressed as a sequence of operations rooted in particular collections. Thus, order inversion implies a total reconstruction of the query and misses optimization choices. If a database is designed using a single collection of complex objects, one must pay special attention to how the query language allows to access and manipulate objects 'parts'. If an arbitrary collection contains documents with one or more arrays comprised of JSON Objects, projecting a subset of the latter and then flattening can be done by following two approaches: (1) deconstruct the array field/s and discard documents not complying with a given condition c; (2) evaluate the c against the objects within the array field in a projection and return new documents with an array containing only the elements that matched the condition, then deconstruct. Option 2 has the advantage of reducing the load over the array deconstruction phase by passing subsets of the original arrays to it: 2 performed better than 1 in our experiments. Query plans indicate that MongoDB's optimizer does not consider this fact as to restructure a query. Our view is that selection of complex objects is ambiguous. For instance, it is possible to select the customers where some embedded order fulfills a certain condition. Depending on the query, two different types of output are sought: the customer object as is (with all embedded orders), and the customer object with *only those orders that fulfilled the condition*. Implementing separate operators for each case may lead to better performance. In document stores, optimization resides on whoever writes the query: MongoDB and (especially) Couchbase being representatives of document stores show how these systems lack an optimizer capable of effectively re-ordering predicates.

· The optimal ordering of operations on collections depends on the schema of the collections. Query 22 is an example of this. Using one combination helped decrease the running time of the query on S.2, but did the opposite for the query on S.1. There are two optimizations that would help decrease running time, but are not carried out: (1) Whenever q selects elements after their deconstruction from an array the query planner could opt to transform such sequence into a projection that filters the elements within the array first, then deconstructs. (2) Whenever q has a join, the query planner could opt to change the direction of it. However, transforming a left outer join into a right outer join or vice-versa

---

[4] See https://forums.couchbase.com/t/correlated-subquery-with-two-buckets/ 25160/12.

would prove to be difficult as, in the worst case, the entire query needs to be rewritten. · Certain query patterns are especially problematic for documents and, because of this, the use of more advanced operators without a SQL counterpart become necessary. A query from either S.1, S.2, or S.3 may require self-joins– query 22 in MongoDB has an uncorrelated sub-query that translates to this and in Couchbase's recommended setup every join is a self-join. The experiments have shown this approach has a detrimental impact on schemas S.2 and S.3. This shows (1) the concept of *self-join* known from RDBMSs does not translate well to document systems, particularly on navigational languages, and (2) it is quite problematic to translate complex SQL queries into these systems.

3   Conclusions and Further Research

We have described an experiment to compare a relational database (PostgreSQL) to NoSQL document stores (MongoDB, Couchbase) in the context of Decision Support (DSS). We design and implement the experiment using the TPCH benchmark, and examine the influence of database design and query language optimization on performance. We have shown that the typical document store design is not always a good fit for DSS environments and that navigational languages must be supported by a sophisticated optimizer that is able to rewrite and reorder operations in a query in order to extract the best performance possible. We stress that both MongoDB and Couchbase are evolving systems. Therefore, our criticism should be understood as suggestions to guide future development. Future work includes extending the comparison to column-oriented databases and exploring the storage of document as multi-dimensional arrays, plus considering further schemas and query sets.

References

1. Abiteboul, S., Bidoit, N.: Non first normal form relations: an algebra allowing data restructuring. J. Comput. Syst. Sci. 33(3), 361–393 (1986)
2. Floratou, A., Teletia, N., DeWitt, D.J., Patel, J.M., Zhang, D.: Can the elephants handle the NoSQL onslaught? Proc. VLDB Endow. 5(12), 1712–1723 (2012)
3. Kamsky, A.: Adapting TPC-C benchmark to measure performance of multi-document transactions in MongoDB. In: Proceedings of the 29th VLDB Conference (2019)
4. McSherry, F., Isard, M., Murray, D.G.: Scalability! But at what cost? In: 15th Workshop on Hot Topics in Operating Systems (HotOS 2015) (2015)
5. Parker, Z., Poe, S., Vrbsky, S.V.: Comparing NoSQL MongoDB to an SQL DB. In: Proceedings of the 51st ACM Southeast Conference, ACMSE 2013, pp. 5:1–5:6. ACM, New York (2013). https://doi.org/10.1145/2498328.2500047. http://doi.acm.org/10.1145/2498328.2500047
6. Specification, Standard and TPC, Transaction Processing Performance Council: TPC BENCHMARK TM H. Standard, San Francisco, CA, September 2017

A Framework for Supporting Repetition and Evaluation in the Process of Cloud-Based DBMS Performance Benchmarking

Patrick K. Erdelt[✉]

Beuth Hochschule fuer Technik Berlin, Luxemburger Strasse 10,
13353 Berlin, Germany
patrick.erdelt@beuth-hochschule.de

Abstract. Performance benchmarking of Database Management Systems (DBMS) is an important yet complicated process. We motivate and present two supporting Python packages which help to avoid common pitfalls and in particular improve reproducibility and transparency in heterogeneous systems with hardware accelerators. The first addresses operational aspects by providing dynamic testbeds using Docker images, especially for cloud-based systems. The second helps planning and recurrently running experiments in a predefined setup via JDBC/SQL, and analyzing results with automated reports and an interactive dashboard. The purpose of this is to thoroughly evaluate aspects of performances of DBMS based on real-life measurements, runtime and hardware metrics, depending on various parameters including the hardware, and with high repeatability. We present a series of TPC-H inspired example benchmarks in a Kubernetes cluster for demonstration, and some lessons learned.

Keywords: Database Management Systems · Performance evaluation · Benchmarking · Virtualization · Docker · Cloud-based systems · Kubernetes · Resource consumption · GPU · CPU · Tools

1 Introduction

DBMS performance benchmarks are used by DBMS developers to evaluate their work and to find out which algorithm works best in which situation. Benchmarks are used by (potential) customers to evaluate what system or hardware to buy or rent. Benchmarks are used by administrators to find bottlenecks and adjust configurations. Benchmarks are used by users to compare semantically equivalent queries and to find the best formulation alternative. All of these interest groups may want to change a parameter and rerun the benchmark. Results will depend on data (structure, size, cardinality of attributes) and queries (complexity, components like projection, restriction, aggregation, sorting), but also hardware, configuration of software (server settings or DDL parameter) and the

© Springer Nature Switzerland AG 2021
R. Nambiar and M. Poess (Eds.): TPCTC 2020, LNCS 12752, pp. 75–92, 2021.
https://doi.org/10.1007/978-3-030-84924-5_6

number and behaviour of clients. In an ideal situation the process of benchmarking workload W is performed as: 1. Perform n benchmark runs using (hardware and software) configurations γ_1 to γ_n, where γ_i are completely on display, 2. Evaluate results statistically and drill-down on interesting aspects. We identify the need for a framework 1. to support the process; that is providing dynamic testbeds by helping to create, manage and monitor experiment setups using Docker images for virtualization, optionally in a High-Performance-Computing (HPC) cluster environment, 2. to collect all data that could be relevant to evaluate and classify results, including system information. Inspired by what is now called Data Science, where it is common to build a workflow pipeline and to inspect collected data visually and statistically for patterns and anomalies, we motivate Python as the scripting language for all tasks.

1.1   Contributions

In the following we carry out considerations that motivated design decisions for two benchmarking tools, DBMSBenchmarker[1] and Bexhoma[2], available as open-source Python packages under AGPL-3.0 license. We also refer to other Python packages that are helpful in this context. We sketch a series of experiments we have run to check feasibility and potential. We also present some lessions learned, in particular about 1. using Docker images 2. using monitoring 3. in a Kubernetes (K8s) cluster.

DBMSBenchmarker is a Python3-based application-level black box benchmarking tool for DBMS. It connects to a given list of DBMS (via JDBC) and runs a given list of (SQL) queries. Queries can be parametrized and randomized. It

- investigates timing aspects - connection, execution, data transfer
- computes derived metrics - in total, per session, throughput, latency, etc.
- investigates statistics - sensitive and resistant to outliers
- investigates other aspects - received result sets, hardware metrics, etc.
- helps to evaluate results in multidimensional analysis - by providing Python data structures, statistics, plots, Latex reporting and an interactive inspection tool.

Bexhoma helps managing DBMS benchmarking experiments in a HPC cluster environment. It enables users to configure hardware/software setups for easier execution of tests over varying configurations, different hardware, DBMS, DBMS configurations, DB settings, etc. The basic workflow (Fig. 1) is:

- start a virtual machine
- install monitoring software and a DBMS as Docker containers
- import data
- run benchmarks (using DBMSBenchmarker) and
- shut down everything with a single command.

---

[1] https://github.com/Beuth-Erdelt/DBMS-Benchmarker.
[2] https://github.com/Beuth-Erdelt/Benchmark-Experiment-Host-Manager.

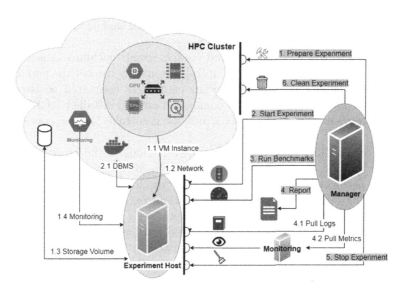

Fig. 1. Testbed workflow

A more advanced workflow is: Plan a sequence of such experiments, run plan as a batch and join results for comparison. The workflow is stored for repetition and protocol. The tool supports K8s and AWS.

1.2   Related Work

In [16] the authors present a cloud-centric analysis of eight evaluation frameworks. Some observations are 1. only a few frameworks support visualisation 2. only OLTP-Bench [7] considers resource monitoring 3. none provides cloud orchestration tools. In [4] the authors inspect several frameworks, in particular YCSB [6] and OLTP-Bench, collect requirements for a DBMS benchmarking framework in an interview based method and per interest group, and report their findings. Among others, existing problems are 1. time-consuming initial setup and configuration 2. lack of metadata collection 3. too laborious to do statistical analysis. The conclusions are quite similar to our starting point. The authors plead in favour of a holistic approach and list as major requirements for a framework to be developed: • Generality and versatility • Extensibility and abstraction • Usability and configurability • Track everything • Repeatability/reproducibility. In [14] the authors explain common pitfalls in DBMS performance benchmarking. They also provide a checklist how to avoid these pitfalls. They stress the importance of • reproducibility (availability of hardware configuration, DBMS parameters and version, source code or binary files) • a close inspection of hot vs. warm vs. cold data • ensuring correctness • using different data and various workloads • doing several runs to reduce interference • using robust metrics (standard deviation, median and confidence intervals). One conclusion is to use virtual machine images. We hope to provide a starting point for benchmarking users to avoid some of the pitfalls and to meet some of the requirements with our solution.

The performance of virtualized and containerized machines in general is a subject of research, for example [1,2]. In [15] the authors inspect the performance of one specific DBMS running in Docker containers compared to baremetal. DBMSBenchmarker uses JDBC to connect to any preinstalled RDBMS, so it could be helpful in such comparisons, but we here take Docker containers as given.

We do not consider automated stopping criterions or the process as closed-loop otherwise, but it may be fruitful to refine this direction: In [10] the authors introduce a performance testing methodology for cloud applications. They note that due to the random performance fluctuations extensive (and costly) benchmarking seems necessary. They provide a statistics-based criterion to determine when to stop testing early. In [11] the authors introduce a framework SQLScalpel for DBMS performance benchmarking. It helps to inspect a (very big) query space dynamically based on a query grammar. The authors consider everything fixed except for the queries, when we, in this report, contrarily consider the workload fixed and some other parameters varying.

1.3   Motivation

An (in)famous bonmot about DBMS benchmarking says it's always possible to construct a benchmark showing the result you want to have. This situation has led to standardized benchmarks like the TPC family and Yahoo! Cloud Serving Benchmark. These benchmarks are highly accepted, actively supported and elaborated in detail. Standardized benchmarks like TPC-H help a lot when it comes to evaluating DBMS. We think the bonmot is true, but not a drawback but a benefit. It is tempting to have one single metric, a single number to determine what is the one best DBMS. One single metric on the other hand means very high aggregation and coarse evaluation. To have more insight and to have a better understanding of the differences, we want to analyze metrics and drill-down on certain aspects. This suggests collecting fine-grained measurements, that is, to measure each single step of processing in addition to hardware metrics. Some basic derived metrics should be analysis of outliers in runtime, influence of warmup and cooldown phases and (re)connections, exploration of performance bottlenecks and the latency-throughput tradeoff (i.e. influence of number of clients). We deduce a framework should **R1** *provide detailed data and evaluations in a usable format for performance debugging*.

One can identify three stages in the benchmarking workflow: 1. Preprocess: Deploy experiment, possibly in a cloud 2. Process: Run predefined benchmarks and collect as much data about the system as possible 3. Postprocess: Statistical evaluation of results in a handy and common output format. We believe this is not a purely linear once and for all pipeline. We deduce a framework should help **R2** *rerunning the process for reproducibility or with varying parameters to analyze dependencies*. We also deduce a framework should be based on a **R3** *common and powerful scripting language for defining the benchmark processes and for evaluating results.*

It is common to have several DBMS for different purposes. The classical row-wise and disk-placed general purpose Relational DBMS still is very important, mostly due to ACID for OLTP requirements and very sophisticated and mature products, for example MariaDB, MS SQL Server, MySQL, Oracle Database and PostgreSQL. With the rise of analytical (OLAP) workloads and later Self-BI requirements have changed. High cardinality, subqueries, not necessarily normalized tables, data warehouses, star scheme, descriptive statistics on columns and more complex computations of metrics and KPIs have come to focus. Column-wise treatment of data and In-Memory DBMS have shown to be appropriate. The requirements can be tackled by tailored engines for the above DBMS and there are also specialized DBMS like Exasol, MemSQL and MonetDB. However more memory is needed and CPU intense tasks like parallel execution and decompression of columns put further demand on hardware, and this also affects GPUs. GPU-enhanced DBMS have been subject of research for more than 10 years, in particular when it comes to classical DBMS areas like query optimization, filter, sort and JOIN. Bress et al. gave a survey in 2014 [5]. There are also some commercial vendors, such as Brytlyt, Kinetica, OmniSci and SQreamDB. GPUs in general become more and more interesting: Heavy parallel computation capabilities, the end of Moore's law, dropping prices of GPUs and their increasing prevalence, mainly due to Deep Learning applications. On the other hand GPUs still make hardware more expensive and one wouldn't use them if they are not proven to be helpful. We deduce a framework should **R4** *include a broad spectrum of DBMS, accessed by a unified interface.*

Surely performance depends on hardware components. The diversity of DBMS, even in a Relational context alone, suggests different demand for CPU, RAM and GPU. We thus want the framework to **R5** *help in monitoring resource consumption and to collect data about the host.* A HPC cluster is supposed to be the right environment to pick scalable hardware configurations, that is flexibility, elasticity and cost-aware solutions for Infrastructure as a Service (IaaS). We deduce a framework should **R6** *help deployment of experiments in a cloud,* but also have **R7** *management of experimental setup, actual benchmarking and evaluation of results as separate steps,* since one may or may not use a cloud service.

1.4 Solution Concept

In the previous section we collected requirements for a benchmarking framework. In the following we reason how these requirements can be met by our design decisions.

Python. Requirement **R3** alone already strongly suggests to use Python. Moreover Python is the de-facto programming language for data analysis in a Data Science setting. Also, we can comply with **R1** and **R2** by using standard Python

R	Requirement	D	Design
R1	Detailed Evaluation	D1	Python - Reporting, Interactive Dashboard
R2	Reproducibility	D2	Python - Configuration Dictionaries
R3	Scripting Language	D3	Python
R4	All of the above DBMS	D4	Docker, JDBC
R5	Collect Resource Consumption	D5	Monitoring - Prometheus/Grafana
R6	Workflow Management	D6	Docker, K8s, AWS
R7	As Optional	D7	Separate Python modules

data structures like Dictionaries and DataFrames for configurations and results. There are a lot of Python packages available to help this approach. 1. `boto3` and `kubernetes` for cluster management 2. `JayDeBeApi` and `JPype1` for JDBC connections 3. for automated collection of experiment information: `paramiko`, `scp`, `urllib3`, `psutil`, `requests` 4. for evaluations: `numpy`, `pandas`, `scipy`, `matplotlib`, `plotly`, `dash`. All of the DBMS mentioned above provide a JDBC driver. JDBC is flexible and reliable enough to be a communication interface for a lot of applications, BI tools and programming languages, including Python, and thus is accurate for representing the actual usage.

Virtualization. Virtualization is a common practise and forms one basis for cloud computing. A state-of-the-art way to deploy software is using Docker for containerization. All of the DBMS mentioned above provide a Docker image. It is easy to derive own images if one wants to change configuration. It is also easy to receive a clean copy installation (but this does not affect the host cache [15]). Reproducibility and portability are very high, since an image contains all information about the installation and Docker is available for many systems. Containerized images are publically hosted by vendors and adding a layer containing changes requires a small amount of extra data. Although one can expect some loss of performance [1,2], and loss depends on the type of resource, we propose that using the same type of virtualization for all DBMS yields a fair situation. Moreover it is best practise to include changes for example concerning compiler flags or server settings in a Dockerfile, that is, basically in a text file. In the end it is a founding concern to have all configurations inside of the image to ensure maximum reproducibility in case a restart is necessary. Hence we decide **D4** *to use Docker containers and JDBC* to fulfill **R4**.

Using Kubernetes for orchestration of containers is on the rise. AWS is a big market player in IaaS not only for evaluation but also for productional use. It is common practise to use cloud services, but performance is not completely stable and evaluation needs additional statistical treatment [10], that is, at least, recurring runs of the same benchmark. We hence want to meet **R6** by **D6** *using Docker containers and providing support for managing experiments in AWS and K8s clouds*. We decide to meet **R7** by splitting up the framework into two modules, one for managing experiments in a cloud environment and one for performing benchmarking when an experiment is already set up. This allows 1.

to analyze a DBMS outside of a cluster 2. to only do experiment setup, and benchmark the installed DBMS using any other tool.

Contrarily to most other tools, we assume data generation happens externally and all DBMS share the same source of CSV files. We aim at performing a lot of sequential repetitions of the same workload, so always mounting the same volume having the raw data avoids time consuming traffic to the cluster. For standard benchmarks there are sophisticated generation tools around.

We want to meet **R5** by **D5** *using Prometheus/Grafana for monitoring*, since it is a common practise in cluster management. There are exporters to monitor resource usage like CPU, RAM, GPU [9,12,13]. Monitoring is less invasive and much easier and schematic to implement than (the more precise) profiling and less diverse and easier to reuse than logging. Apriori, it treats a DBMS as a black box. We can use Python to collect metrics from Grafana. Moreover there are vendor specific extension to gain deeper insight.

2   Experiments

We run a series of experiments on a K8s cluster to 1. illustrate the workflow 2. show it is feasible to see characteristics in runtime and resource consumption 3. quantify if the same task yields same result each time. The first experiment compares four DBMS and the second inspects monitoring more closely.

Workload. The series of experiments uses some TPC-H queries (SF $= 1$): Q1, Q5–Q7, Q9–Q13. Not all DBMS are capable of all queries, so to obfuscate the DBMS we have made a selection. We further have made a selection due to limited space. Data is present as CSV files inside the cluster on a persistent Ceph volume that is mounted into the containers. The workload W_n is given as the sequence of these queries, each repeated n times before going to the next to have some statistical confidence. To improve assignment of monitored hardware metrics to a query, we also add a parameter d. This contains a delay in seconds before going to the next query.

DBMS. We inspect four DBMS: In-Memory, GPU-enhanced, General Purpose, Columnwise. The Docker images we have used are (almost) as of vendors publicly provided without any optimizations. We added a layer that creates a folder to check derivation of own images is feasible. Data types are chosen basic but typical for each DBMS (for example some use dictionary encoding), so the following is not about obtaining optimal performance but to illustrate the power of the approach. We do not explicitly create any indexes.

Each of the runs of a query may have different parameters due to random-ization, but all DBMS receive the same list of parameters in the same order. All DBMS are queried via Python/JDBC and we receive data in the same format. We then limit precision to 4 decimals (Q1: to 0) to avoid alarming due to different numerical treatment. After sorting all columns we presumably receive the exact same table each time the same parameters are used. At some queries (Q1, Q9, Q10, Q11, Q13) we only store and compare a hash code of the result tables to save RAM. We automatically let the software verify we have obtained the same result sets as expected in the first experiment.

Pods. A DBMS is represented by a K8s pod, that is a collection of Docker containers sharing the host and a network space. A pod also has attached a K8s service for fixing a common network access and to provide a standard interface, so all configurations appear to be the same to the outside world (i.e. the benchmarking instance) and internals are transparent. The pods have two or three containers: 1. The DBMS 2. Google's cAdvisor for monitoring CPU, RAM, network and disk [9] 3. optionally NVidia's DCGM for monitoring GPUs [12].

In the end we have a black box pod, that exposes hardware metrics and a JDBC interface on fixed ports, no matter what the concrete DBMS or host is. A pod is created from a YAML configuration file and it's parameters can easily be manipulated in Python.

Parameters. Benchmarking is a highly parametrized process. In the following we will focus on • workload size n • delay d • DBMS • processor type • CPU/RAM allowed maximum (limit). Other interesting parameters we consider fixed in the following are • number of parallel connections • number of reconnections • CPU/RAM guaranteed minimum (request). Note that K8s reacts to exceeding CPU limit by throttling and to exceeding RAM limit by eviction.

Metrics and Multidimensional Analysis. As a result we obtain measured times in milliseconds for the query processing parts: connection, execution, data transfer. These are described in three dimensions: number of run (query dimension $\mathcal{D}_q$), number of query (workload dimension $\mathcal{D}_w$) and number of configuration (experiment dimension $\mathcal{D}_e$). The configurations γ_j consist of various parameters like DBMS, selected processor, assigned cluster node, number of clients and execution order. We also have various hardware metrics like CPU and GPU utilization, CPU throttling, memory caching and working set. These are also described in three dimensions: Second of query execution time (time dimension $\mathcal{D}_t$), $\mathcal{D}_w$ and $\mathcal{D}_e$. All these metrics can be sliced or diced, rolled-up or drilled-down into the various dimensions using several aggregation functions. A change of aggregation of $\mathcal{D}_e$ for instance can yield metrics per DBMS. We also compute query latency (sum of connection, execution and data transfer time).

First Experiment: Compare DBMS. We want to compare the performances of four DBMS and obtain some idea about the statistical confidence. In order to do so, we run the workload W_{64} without delay eight times: Four DBMS, each having a processor selected, process the workload twice without reinstall. The received result sets should be compared automatically. We limit CPU to 4 hyperthreads to have a mild but noticeable limitation. Figure 2. shows the experiment setup conceptually.

Workload: W_{64}, $d = 0$

Config	DBMS	Processor	Install	Data	CPU Limit
γ_1	In-Memory	AMD EPYC 7542	true	true	4
γ_2	In-Memory	AMD EPYC 7542	false	true	4
γ_3	General-Purpose	AMD EPYC 7542	true	true	4
γ_4	General-Purpose	AMD EPYC 7542	false	true	4
γ_5	Columnwise	AMD EPYC 7542	true	true	4
γ_6	Columnwise	AMD EPYC 7542	false	true	4
γ_7	GPU-enhanced	NVIDIA V100	true	true	4
γ_8	GPU-enhanced	NVIDIA V100	false	true	4

Fig. 2. First experiment: compare 4 DBMS

Bexhoma translates this into eight YAML files and creates eight K8s pods one after the other. DBMSBenchmarker benchmarks the performance of these black box pods and collects data. Some key observations (Fig. 3) are:

Figure 3(a) GPU-enhanced is fastest, General-Purpose is clearly slowest. The plot shows the macro averages of query latencies, averaged per DBMS.

Figure 3(b) In-Memory is fastest. The plot shows means (per DBMS) of geometric means (per workload) of mean query latencies (per run).

Figure 3(c) GPU-enhanced is slowest in connecting. The plot drills-down Fig. 3(b) to query parts and normalizes per query to 1 (= fastest = lowest mean).

Figure 3(d) The second run of the workload is executed always faster than the first one, GPU-enhanced and In-Memory benefit most. The plot drills-down Fig. 3(c) to the single configurations γ_1 to γ_8 in $\mathcal{D}_e$.

Let's look at a per query view:

Figure 4(a) In-Memory excels at executing Q6 and Q11, GPU-enhanced at Q7 and Q9. The plot drills-down Fig. 3(d) to the queries, limited to the second workload, two DBMS and execution. On the GPU-enhanced, execution of Q6 and Q11 takes about ten times as long as on the In-Memory.

Figure 4(b) At some queries the GPU-enhanced clearly stabilizes in the second run.

Figure 4(c) In-Memory has a high variation at Q6. The difference to the previous plot is this one is more sensitive to outliers and thus better indicates anomalic behaviour. This plot ignores the first (warmup) run of each query, which has a natural high variation.

Figure 4(d) Warmup affects execution time and there seems to be some kind of caching active at the GPU-enhanced. The plot shows the n execution times of Q9. The upper lines are the instances of the In-Memory, the lower lines are of the GPU-enhanced. The parameters of run 13, 16, 23, 24 asf. happen to be duplicates of previous runs.

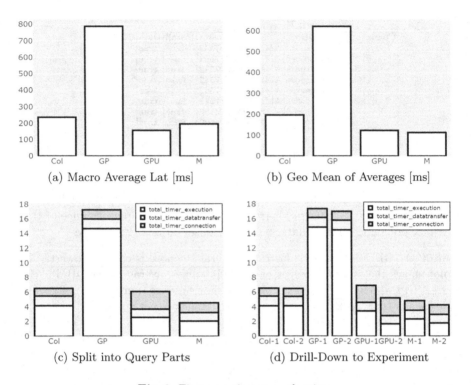

(a) Macro Average Lat [ms]

(b) Geo Mean of Averages [ms]

(c) Split into Query Parts

(d) Drill-Down to Experiment

Fig. 3. First experiment: evaluation

Figure 4(e)   Columnwise is fastest in the first run of the workload, GPU-enhanced is slowest. Aggregation to only the first runs (in $\mathcal{D}_q$) yields a picture very different from 4(d). General purpose and Columnwise are not affected much by repetition. GPU-enhanced has a long warmup phase.

We observe the definition of *fastest* very much depends on the aggregation function, the query and the number of run.

We also see Q6 has a very high variation in terms of cv (Fig. 4(c)), so we get the impression something is wrong. Indeed it turns out due to a mistake in randomization of query parameters we have a lot of (correct) empty result sets at Q6 and this system reacts sensitively. Q6 does not contain a GROUP BY and queries a single table. This seems to be ideal for the In-Memory (Fig. 4(a)). Q7 and Q9 have a rather big JOIN of 6 tables in a subquery that is aggregated afterwards using several GROUP BY. Moreover Q9 involves 4 columns in a computation and this is computationally intense (in particular for the Columnwise - Fig. 5). Apparently the GPU-enhanced is very good at this situation (Fig. 4(a)). To further pin down specific choke points [3,8] and to quantify their effect we

	Q1	Q5	Q6	Q7	Q9	Q10	Q11	Q12	Q13
M-2	1.04	1.37	1.0	6.06	12.72	1.56	1.0	1.0	1.34
GPU-2	1.0	1.0	10.44	1.0	1.0	1.0	9.12	1.2	1.0

(a) Normalized Mean Execution Latency, First run ignored

	Q1	Q5	Q6	Q7	Q9	Q10	Q11	Q12	Q13
M-2	8.48	3.85	8.06	2.33	12.56	23.44	5.1	37.48	3.1
M-1	24.96	7.27	7.88	1.19	11.68	23.25	3.76	39.39	1.95
GPU-2	2.62	1.94	6.16	2.52	3.16	4.19	3.17	4.44	31.18
GPU-1	8.75	5.72	4.81	3.1	69.34	61.46	55.83	4.53	48.1

(b) Quartile Coefficient of Dispersion (qcod) of Execution Latencies [%]

	Q1	Q5	Q6	Q7	Q9	Q10	Q11	Q12	Q13
M-2	20.13	10.01	126.71	10.39	19.29	24.88	7.92	38.3	11.48
M-1	71.37	25.65	183.08	22.06	23.93	36.76	125.04	48.64	5.23
GPU-2	6.28	7.24	11.04	9.78	6.92	6.13	7.87	9.77	32.22
GPU-1	16.01	10.23	9.08	8.43	53.12	73.85	65.72	8.4	101.81

(c) Coefficient of Variation (cv) of Execution Latencies, First run ignored [%]

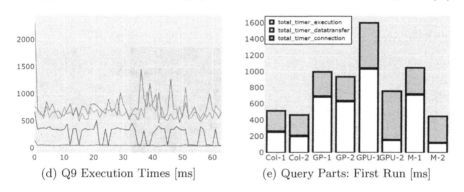

(d) Q9 Execution Times [ms]   (e) Query Parts: First Run [ms]

Fig. 4. First experiment: evaluation continued

could widen the query space or prepare other Docker images containing the same DBMS with different settings, and rerun the experiment.

Let's look at some hardware metrics per query and configuration in Fig. 5.

Figure 5(a)   CPU utilization depends on the query, but in general Columnwise and In-Memory use the most and GPU-enhanced uses the least.

Figure 5(b)   GPU-enhanced and General Purpose are (almost) not throttled, but Columnwise and In-Memory are heavily.

Figure 5(c)   GPU-enhanced uses most (CPU-)RAM, Columnwise is apparently the only DBMS which frees memory here.

	Col-1	Col-2	GP-1	GP-2	GPU-1	GPU-2	M-1	M-2
Q13	1.88	1.53	2.73	2.7	2.88	1.55	2.63	3.42
Q12	2.41	1.77	2.8	2.88	0.67	1.61	0.37	0.3
Q11	1.19	1.4	1.59	1.74	1.57	1.8	5.06	3.87
Q10	3.54	3.12	2.69	2.73	1.42	0.48	4.27	3.45
Q9	4.12	4.03	2.8	2.7	1.49	1.17	3.73	3.86
Q7	3.56	2.94	2.77	2.74	1.27	0.85	3.42	3.08
Q6	3.31	3.18	2.68	3.16	1.66	0.93	2.73	3.22
Q5	3.39	3.82	2.85	2.92	1.68	0.43	3.4	3.22
Q1	3.41	3.66	2.59	2.94	0.9	0.04	0.07	0.04

(a) Median of CPU Utilization

	Col-1	Col-2	GP-1	GP-2	GPU-1	GPU-2	M-1	M-2
Q13	0.04	0.0	0.0	0.0	8.7	0.58	1.9	1.53
Q12	0.42	0.08	0.0	0.0	0.02	0.01	0.0	0.0
Q11	0.37	0.28	0.0	0.0	0.0	0.05	5.16	3.59
Q10	1.64	3.83	0.0	0.0	0.0	0.0	3.17	1.94
Q9	21.97	20.88	0.0	0.0	0.04	0.0	2.29	2.31
Q7	5.32	4.29	0.0	0.0	0.0	0.0	9.25	4.28
Q6	4.38	4.66	0.0	0.0	0.0	0.0	4.22	2.08
Q5	2.07	1.89	0.0	0.0	0.0	0.0	3.35	2.08
Q1	2.03	2.66	0.0	0.0	0.0	0.0	0.0	0.0

(b) Median of CPU Throttling

	Col-1	Col-2	GP-1	GP-2	GPU-1	GPU-2	M-1	M-2
Q13	1.53	1.56	1.51	1.52	3.27	3.43	1.93	2.01
Q12	1.5	1.49	1.49	1.5	3.17	3.43	1.86	2.0
Q11	1.45	1.45	1.49	1.5	3.17	3.43	1.85	2.0
Q10	1.44	1.6	1.5	1.52	3.12	3.41	1.84	2.0
Q9	1.44	1.73	1.5	1.52	3.08	3.41	1.79	2.0
Q7	1.36	1.72	1.32	1.51	2.95	3.42	1.53	2.0
Q6	1.2	1.67	1.28	1.49	2.79	3.41	1.42	2.0
Q5	1.42	1.65	1.29	1.5	2.52	3.41	1.37	2.0
Q1	0.77	1.85	1.06	1.49	1.93	3.41	1.23	2.0

(c) Median of RAM Usage [GiB]

Fig. 5. First experiment: evaluation of hardware metrics

We observe monitoring has limited reliability at some queries. We have almost none CPU utilization at Q1 for In-Memory in Fig. 5(b). Monitoring only scrapes metrics every few seconds, so we have to increase number of runs to be more sure we really matched the dimensions $\mathcal{D}_t$ and $\mathcal{D}_q$, that is a hardware metric representative for the query. We will do so in the second experiment.

Second Experiment: Inspect In-Memory. We now want to inspect the resource consumption of the In-Memory DBMS in execution more closely. In order to do so, we run the workload W_{1024} with a delay of 60s fifty times: The DBMS processes the workload ten times with reinstall on each of five different processors. We refrain from receiving result sets since this yields time gaps between query executions and we (again) only connect once per workload query. Figure 6 shows the experiment setup conceptually.

Workload: W_{1024}, $d = 60$

Config	DBMS	Processor	Install	Data	CPU Limit
γ_1	In-Memory	AMD EPYC 7542	true	false	∞
...	...	...	...	...	...
γ_{11}	In-Memory	Intel(R) Xeon CPU E5-2630 v3	true	false	∞
...	...	...	...	...	...
γ_{21}	In-Memory	Intel(R) Xeon CPU E5-2630 v4	true	false	∞
...	...	...	...	...	...
γ_{31}	In-Memory	Intel(R) Xeon Silver 4110 CPU	true	false	∞
...	...	...	...	...	...
γ_{41}	In-Memory	AMD Opteron Processor 6378	true	false	∞
...	...	...	...	...	...
γ_{50}	In-Memory	AMD Opteron Processor 6378	true	false	∞

Fig. 6. Second experiment: In-Memory DBMS on different CPUs

We can verify (plots not included), that no throttling takes place and same processor means same host node in the cluster. Some other key observations are:

Figure 7(a) Execution Performance is best on EPYC 7542, does not vary much between the. two E5-2630 and is lowest on Opteron 6378. The plot shows the means (per CPU) of the geometric means (per workload) of means of execution latencies (per query).

Figure 7(b) Execution Performance is very stable, varying less than 1.5%. The plot shows the coefficients of variation (per CPU) of geometric means (per workload) of means of execution latencies (per query).

Let's look at a per query view:

Figure 7(c) Q6 and Q11 are fast, EPYC 7542 is fastest for all queries.

Figure 7(d) CPU utilization is more characteristic for the query than the processor.

Figure 7(e) Variation of maximum latencies is still high at Q6. The plot shows a slice of the qcod (per CPU) of the max execution latencies per query.

Figure 7(f) Variation of maximum CPU is low. The plot shows a slice of the qcod (per CPU) of the max CPU utilizations per query.

Again the DBMS is very good at Q6 and Q11. We now also see this does not come from heavy CPU utilization. Costly are in particular Q1 (computations involving four different columns, two GROUP BY), Q10 (seven GROUP BY) and again Q9.

3 Lessons Learned

Monitoring and Host Metrics in a Kubernetes Cluster. It is feasible to monitor resource consumption using Prometheus/Grafana in an automated way. This not only applies to monitoring a cluster or it's nodes, but also allows a per container inspection. It is also possible to monitor the monitoring container costs (about 0.5 CPU), so this method is invasive but bearable. Due to limited space we have not included all examples in this paper, like GPU, VRAM, network and disk

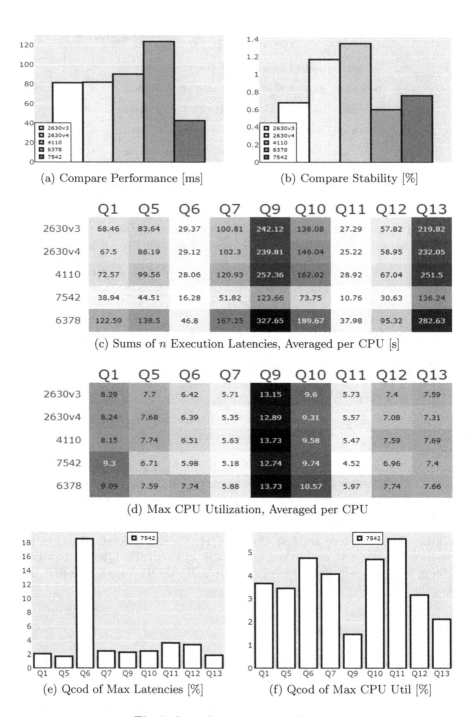

(a) Compare Performance [ms]

(b) Compare Stability [%]

(c) Sums of n Execution Latencies, Averaged per CPU [s]

	Q1	Q5	Q6	Q7	Q9	Q10	Q11	Q12	Q13
2630v3	68.46	83.64	29.37	100.81	242.12	138.08	27.29	57.82	219.82
2630v4	67.5	86.19	29.12	102.3	239.81	146.04	25.22	58.95	232.05
4110	72.57	99.56	28.06	120.93	257.36	162.02	28.92	67.04	251.5
7542	38.94	44.51	16.28	51.82	123.66	73.75	10.76	30.63	136.24
6378	122.59	138.5	46.8	167.25	327.65	189.67	37.98	95.32	282.63

(d) Max CPU Utilization, Averaged per CPU

	Q1	Q5	Q6	Q7	Q9	Q10	Q11	Q12	Q13
2630v3	8.29	7.7	6.42	5.71	13.15	9.6	5.73	7.4	7.59
2630v4	8.24	7.68	6.39	5.35	12.89	9.31	5.57	7.08	7.31
4110	8.15	7.74	6.51	5.63	13.73	9.58	5.47	7.59	7.69
7542	9.3	6.71	5.98	5.18	12.74	9.74	4.52	6.96	7.4
6378	9.09	7.59	7.74	5.88	13.73	10.57	5.97	7.74	7.66

(e) Qcod of Max Latencies [%]

(f) Qcod of Max CPU Util [%]

Fig. 7. Second experiment: evaluation

usage and CPU utilization by other processes and thus general host workload. Monitoring suggests stress tests, since queries often happen in a subsecond scale and monitoring on the other hand typically scrapes metrics only every few (here: 5) seconds. Moreover processor usage is more volatile than RAM. We have used Prometheus `irate` to estimate utilization, that computes the difference between the last two measured values (counters), so there is a vagueness of up to 10 s.

Collection of Metadata. We have found it very helpful to have the experiment setups to automatically report as much properties as possible. That is we have

1. the parameters of the experiment
2. node information by asking K8s
3. basic information about the host system by connecting to a running pod.

These can be used as describing dimensions in evaluation of measurements. By attaching labels to nodes of the cluster we can govern the granularity of node selection.

Evaluation. It makes a difference which aggregation function is used. We may want to use

- basics: first, last, min, max, sum
- central tendency and dispersion more sensitive to outliers: arithmetic mean and standard deviation
- and less sensitive to outliers: median and interquartile range.

Moreover we might want to focus on the first wamup run or contrarily leave it out. In a benchmark like TPC-H, where queries can be expected to have very differing query latencies, it is also important to have metrics ignoring the scale like the geometric mean. This in particular holds for heterogeneous systems. We have also used:

- coefficient of variation (cv, dimensionless, in percent)
- quartile coefficient of dispersion (qcod, dimensionless, in percent)
- and a factor relative to the found minimum mean.

Other interesting measures to evaluate results statistically we have not used here are the percentiles. It is helpful to not only look at statistical values, but to also examine the results visually. We have used bar charts, line plots and heatmaps here. Other plots useful for inspecting distributions are histogram and box plot. Each one of these metrics and plots can show it's own insights and we want to be able to change easily when browsing (a lot of) measurements in different dimensions in a powerful scripting language or interactive dashboard.

Inspected DBMS. By just looking at property sheets and compliance to SQL standards we can see GPU-enhanced DBMS are not as mature as well established general purpose systems. But the inspected DBMS performs very well at some TPC-H queries and even outperforms an In-Memory system in a situation without any optimization. Documentation says there is no result caching, so the found effect may indicate caching of the query optimizer. Copying data to GPU takes time. The hot vs. warm vs. cold run problem [14] is prominent. This, to a lesser extend, also holds for the In-Memory system, which can be considered fastest in most queries and in total (as geometric mean). However for ad-hoc (first) queries, the Columnswise is faster. It also can make use of more CPU and apparently frees memory when not used anymore, so it can in this sense deal with resources more efficiently. In the given configuration the General Purpose is not prepared for the TPC-H situation. Verifying installation is important. Last but not least: The process can break down at any step for any reason, so in our experience easy repetition and close inspection is fundamental.

4   Conclusion

In this paper, we have motivated the approach to use Python, JDBC, a cloud service and container-based virtual machines in form of Docker for DBMS performance benchmarking. We briefly have presented a framework to assist in the process and in evaluating the results. Support for deployment in Kubernetes, automation of collection of metrics and descriptive metadata and using monitoring have proven to be feasible and helpful decisions. A Kubernetes pod can be used as a black box exposing metrics and a common communication interface in a handy and transparent way.

We have run some TPC-H inspired experiments to show it is feasible and how to inspect performance aspects. It is particularly important in heterogeneous, cloud-based systems with hardware accelerators to inspect timing aspects and resource consumption closely, to evaluate fine-grained results statistically, and therefore rerun the process several times. As we expect (in an ideal situation) to receive the same result each time we have used some visual and computational techniques for detection and classification of anomalies. We have put our focus primarily on analytical workloads and expect Python to be most representative for this domain. DBMSBenchmarker runs sequences of arbitrary SQL queries, so using DML statements, transactions and stored procedures would be possible, too. To run a benchmark based on operational application logic in the benchmarking instance would need further development though. A promising direction is to benefit from Python's flexibility and enhance DBMSBenchmarker for closed-loop or otherwise adaptive benchmarking.

This project has been partly supported by an AWS Research Grant.

References

1. Arango Gutierrez, C., Dernat, R., Sanabria, J.: Performance evaluation of container-based virtualization for high performance computing environments. Revista UIS Ingenierías **18** (2017). https://doi.org/10.18273/revuin.v18n4-2019003

2. Bachiega, N.G., Souza, P.S.L., Bruschi, S.M., de Souza, S.R.S.: Container-based performance evaluation: a survey and challenges. In: 2018 IEEE International Conference on Cloud Engineering (IC2E), pp. 398–403, April 2018. https://doi.org/10.1109/IC2E.2018.00075

3. Boncz, P., Neumann, T., Erling, O.: TPC-H analyzed: hidden messages and lessons learned from an influential benchmark. In: Nambiar, R., Poess, M. (eds.) TPCTC 2013. LNCS, vol. 8391, pp. 61–76. Springer, Cham (2014). https://doi.org/10.1007/978-3-319-04936-6_5

4. Brent, L., Fekete, A.: A versatile framework for painless benchmarking of database management systems. In: Chang, L., Gan, J., Cao, X. (eds.) ADC 2019. LNCS, vol. 11393, pp. 45–56. Springer, Cham (2019). https://doi.org/10.1007/978-3-030-12079-5_4

5. Breß, S., Heimel, M., Siegmund, N., Bellatreche, L., Saake, G.: GPU-accelerated database systems: survey and open challenges. In: Hameurlain, A., et al. (eds.) Transactions on Large-Scale Data- and Knowledge-Centered Systems XV. LNCS, vol. 8920, pp. 1–35. Springer, Heidelberg (2014). https://doi.org/10.1007/978-3-662-45761-0_1

6. Cooper, B., Silberstein, A., Tam, E., Ramakrishnan, R., Sears, R.: Benchmarking cloud serving systems with YCSB, pp. 143–154, September 2010. https://doi.org/10.1145/1807128.1807152

7. Difallah, D.E., Pavlo, A., Curino, C., Cudre-Mauroux, P.: OLTP-bench: an extensible testbed for benchmarking relational databases. Proc. VLDB Endow. **7**(4), 277–288 (2013). https://doi.org/10.14778/2732240.2732246

8. Dreseler, M., Boissier, M., Rabl, T., Uflacker, M.: Quantifying TPC-H choke points and their optimizations. Proc. VLDB Endow. **13**(10), 1206–1220 (2020). https://doi.org/10.14778/3389133.3389138

9. Google Limited: cadvisor, May 2020. https://github.com/google/cadvisor. Accessed 31 May 2020

10. He, S., Manns, G., Saunders, J., Wang, W., Pollock, L., Soffa, M.L.: A statistics-based performance testing methodology for cloud applications. In: Proceedings of the 2019 27th ACM Joint Meeting on European Software Engineering Conference and Symposium on the Foundations of Software Engineering, ESEC/FSE 2019, pp. 188–199. Association for Computing Machinery, New York (2019). https://doi.org/10.1145/3338906.3338912

11. Kersten, M.L., Koutsourakis, P., Zhang, Y.: Finding the pitfalls in query performance. In: Böhm, A., Rabl, T. (eds.) Proceedings of the 7th International Workshop on Testing Database Systems, DBTest@SIGMOD 2018, Houston, TX, USA, 15 June 2018, pp. 3:1–3:6. ACM (2018). https://doi.org/10.1145/3209950.3209951

12. Nvidia Corporation: NVIDIA Data Center GPU Manager (DCGM), November 2015. https://developer.nvidia.com/dcgm. Accessed 18 May 2019

13. Prometheus: node_exporter, November 2019. https://github.com/prometheus/node_exporter. Accessed 14 Nov 2019

14. Raasveldt, M., Holanda, P., Gubner, T., Mühleisen, H.: Fair benchmarking considered difficult: common pitfalls in database performance testing. In: Proceedings of the Workshop on Testing Database Systems, DBTest 2018, pp. 2:1–2:6. ACM, New York (2018). https://doi.org/10.1145/3209950.3209955

15. Rehmann, K.T., Folkerts, E.: Performance of containerized database management systems. In: Proceedings of the Workshop on Testing Database Systems, DBTest 2018. ACM, New York (2018). https://doi.org/10.1145/3209950.3209953

16. Seybold, D., Domaschka, J.: Is distributed database evaluation cloud-ready? In: Kirikova, M., et al. (eds.) ADBIS 2017. CCIS, vol. 767, pp. 100–108. Springer, Cham (2017). https://doi.org/10.1007/978-3-319-67162-8_12

Benchmarking AI Inference: Where we are in 2020

Miro Hodak, David Ellison, and Ajay Dholakia$^{(\boxtimes)}$

Lenovo, Data Center Group, Morrisville, NC, USA
{mhodak,dellison,adholakia}@lenovo.com

Abstract. AI is continuing to emerge as an important workload across enterprise and academia. Benchmarking is an essential tool to understand its computational requirements and to evaluate performance of different types of accelerators available for AI. However, benchmarking AI inference is complicated as one needs to balance between throughput, latency, and efficiency. Here we survey current state of the field and analyze MLPerf Inference results, which represent the most comprehensive inference performance data available. Additionally, we present our own experience in AI inference benchmarking along with lessons learned in the process. Finally, we offer suggestions for the future we would like to see in AI benchmarking from a point of view of a datacenter server vendor.

Keywords: Artificial intelligence · Inference · MLPerf · Deep learning · GPU · Performance

1 Introduction

AI has seen tremendous growth within the HPC space. The availability of large, labeled datasets and significant increases in computing power have enabled the explosive growth of deep learning (DL) techniques. DL has found use in various tasks such as image classification [1], machine translation [2], and speech processing [3]. Since these DL techniques require significant compute resources, there is a lot of interest in understanding the compute cost of using these techniques and comparing them to one another.

The DL models have two major phases – training and inferencing. The training phase is where the model learns the weights for the neural network that is being trained. The end-to-end process of training a complete neural network can take anywhere from hours to days. Due to this long training time, a lot of effort has been placed into reducing these times either algorithmically or distributing the training across multiple processors or accelerators both within a system or across multiple systems in a cluster. The inference phase is distinctly different. Here, the model is not learning new weights, but just computing them via forward propagation. The inferencing thus takes a sample (e.g. image, phrase) and performs the calculations necessary to classify it. This typically takes fractions of a second and the memory footprint is on the order of megabytes [4].

In practice, inferencing is more complicated than training. It requires a server-like infrastructure and multiple key parameters such as latency, throughput, and efficiency

© Springer Nature Switzerland AG 2021
R. Nambiar and M. Poess (Eds.): TPCTC 2020, LNCS 12752, pp. 93–102, 2021.
https://doi.org/10.1007/978-3-030-84924-5_7

need to be balanced. For example, latency can be improved by performing inference at the edge, but that limits computational power. In terms of AI processing chips, CPUs are useful for the widest variety of models and are the easiest to program, but their processing speed is somewhat limited. Graphical processing units (GPUs) are a common alternative, but they require specialized software and programming. Most existing AI frameworks support GPUs out of the box and/or provide easy-to-use containers, which makes GPUs a practical choice for AI workloads. Another option is Application-Specific Integrated Circuits (ASIC) chips that are built for a specifc purpose. This generally requires custom coding, but if done correctly they can provide high processing speed. A well-know ASIC is a Tensor Processing Unit (TPU) that was developed by Google specifically for DL applications. Currently, there is a lot of interest in this space, with over 100 companies targeting inferencing workloads [5].

Inferencing also needs to balance accuracy with various algorithmic considerations. One popular method for reducing inference time is called network pruning, where a data scientist removes parameters from the network [6]. Another is lowering the numerical precison of model weights, an approach called quantization. This decreases both model storage requirements and inference time. Commonly, a model that is trained at FP32 precision, but is inferenced at FP16 or INT8 precision [7]. This usually causes only small drop in inference accuracy and can be an acceptable trade-off in many situations and currently even lower bit-widths such a 4/2/1-bits are an active field of research [8].

With inferencing there are also multiple scenarios to consider, such the AI workload or how queries are sent to the server. The most common workload is computer vision, which relies on convolutional neural networks, and includes image classification and object detection. The next most common workload is natural language processing, which traditionally involved the use of recurrent neural networks, but now increasingly incorporates transformer-based models. These tasks have different computational characteristics and with multiple patterns of inference requests, the number possible scenarios is considerable.

An effective AI benchmark must either control for or adapt to all the differences in hardware, power, network pruning, and quantization across the different scenarios. Since programming for different hardware requires different code, taking one code base and running it across all systems does not work. For example, code designed for CPUs simply will not work on an ASIC, yet as an industry it is important to be able to fairly compare the two. To deal with these issues a number of inferencing benchmarks have been developed and this work reviews those that have been developed to-date.

This paper starts by covering the state of AI inference benchmarks and highlights the most popular benchmark, MLPerf. Next, we explain the setup and infrastructure needed to perform inference on DL model and give an overview of the sample query methods and categories included MLPerf Inference. We also review results of published MLPerf Inference benchmarks and discuss the upcoming MLPerf Inference v0.7. Finally, we describe our own efforts in inference benchmarking, desribe lessons learned and identify areas that need improvements.

2 Current State of AI Benchmarking

AI benchmarking work in industry as well as academia has been ramping up over the past few years. While performance evaluation of AI workloads has been an active area of research, benchmark development has been a more recent trend. A survey of such recent benchmarking initiatives and evaluation of associated requirements from metrics and system parameters is given in [9].

Initial attempts focued on deep learning model training for computationally intensive tasks like image classification. DeepBench [10] from Baidu Research was one of the early projects and targeted low-level operations such as matrix multiplications and convolutions that are key parts of deep learning algorithms. The goal of DeepBench was to characterize hardware designs best suited for these low-level operations, including communication tasks.

Another project, DAWNBench [11], lead by Stanford University, aimed to evaluate end-to-end deep learning including training and inference stages. The inclusion of AI inference alongside model training in the benchmark scope was driven by the need to address the end-user adoption of AI in the form of using trained models for prediction and other inference scenarios.

MLPerf [12] has emerged as the most popular AI benchmark initiative over the past two years. MLPerf expanded the scope of benchmarking outcome by defining more metrics for a benchmark run to collect and report. Furthermore, the list of tasks included in the benchmark has also been expanded. Starting with a group of enterprises and academic organizations lead by Google, NVIDIA and Intel, the roster of participants has steadily grown [12]. MLPerf appears to be ahead of traditional benchmarking organizations in formulating usable benchmark specifications. The ever growing interest in AI, with its associated complexity, ongoing active research and a shortage of talent to meet the demands are all contributing factors.

MLPerf benchmarks for both training and inference tasks are being released on a periodic cadence. At the time of writing this paper, MLPerf Taining 0.6 is available and Training 0.7 is imminent. Similarly, MLPerf Inference 0.5 is available [13] and Inference 0.7 is expected to be released very soon (version 0.6 is being skipped).

The MLPerf Inference benchmark development is addressing challenges brought on by the need to deal with a large variety in three key areas: models, deployment scenarios and inference systems [13]. Additionally, to ensure that the benchmark is robust against the aforementioned challenges, a set of basic principles was developed to guide the creation of the benchmark. First, a set of representative workloads was selected, including image classification, object detection and translation, and one or more reference models within each are specified. Second, quality targets were defined to meet accuracy within 1% of the reference models. Finally, four realistic end-user scenarios are defined to cover the vast variety of AI inference usage. These guiding principles have enabled a practical and usable benchmark development, attesting to the popularity of MLPerf benchmarks.

However, there are some limitations that need to be understood. The AI tasks addressed by MLPerf are largely deep learning focused. A need also exists to go beyond the training and inference phases of an end-to-end ML workflow. It is important to note that related tasks of data handling and preparation prior to training, and monitoring and continuous learning during inference after initial deployment are also significant in terms of achieving performance, cost and effectiveness measures.

Another active collaboration focused in AI benchmarking is the TPC-AI Workgroup [14, 15]. The Transaction Processing Performance Council (TPC) is an industry initiative created to develop standards and benchmarks for use by vendors, customers and researchers to characterize system performance and total cost of ownership for different types of workloads. TPC benchmarks span a wide spectrum of technologies including transaction processing, decision support systems, data integration, virtualization, big data analytics, internet of things and hyperconverged infrastructure.

TPC defines two classes of benchmarks: Enterprise and Express. Enteprise benchmarks are aimed at characterizing typically complex systems, wherein the benchmark specifications are provided but the implementation is left open for vendors to select based on using commercially available hardware and software products. Express benchmarks, in contrast, are kit-based and require use of the kits to publish benchmark results. Enterprise benchmarks have long development cycles, whereas, as the name suggests, Express benchmarks allow relatively shorter development cycles.

TPC-AI benchmark development work is in progress and is not publically available at this time.

Other notable benchmark development efforts include ADABench [16], an end-to-end ML benchmark proposal that covers the complete ML lifecycle, from data preparation to inference.

3   MLPerf Inference Benchmarking

AI Inference refers to putting a trained model into production. Usually, this involves setting up a service that receives queries and sends back results according the trained model. This means that inference has a different computational profile and requires different metrics to assess performance than training. Throughput and latency are the most important ones, but in practice they have to be balanced with other parameters such as accuracy, memory requirements, computational complexity and power usage. Because of this, inference benchmarking requires more complex infrastructure and evaluation criteria than training.

MLPerf Inference benchmarking infrastructure is shown in Fig. 1. It has several components: LoadGen, a server generating queries and validating responses, SUT (System Under Test), and a Data Set, containing prepared testing data. LoadGen is provided by MLPerf and cannot be changed. It is aware of individual benchmarks and scenarios. SUT is a generalization of the inference system that can respond to queries from the SUT. It can run on a single device (i.e. GPU), entire node with multiple CPU sockets or accelerators, or even on multiple nodes. SUT runs an ML model satisfying MLPerf criteria. Note that by design, submitters are encouraged to customize models to fit their HW and OS toolchain. Certain techniques are prohibited, but in general, submitters have a wide latitude to create their own implementations as long as their model is equivalent to the reference implementation. This decoupling between the traffic generator and the tested system is a key feature of the MLPerf benchmark as it allows fair evaluation of custom implementations of ML workloads.

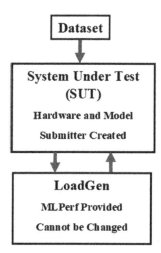

Fig. 1. MLPerf Inference Scheme. MLPerf provides LoadGen server, which cannot be modified, while SUT Inference system is submitter's responsibility.

The system works as follows: First, LoadGen sends a request to the SUT to load data set samples into memory. This "warm-up" action may include compilation and/or data preprocessing and is not counted as a part of the benchmark. Upon finishing the initialization, the SUT sends a signal back to LoadGen, which then starts to send queries according to a selected scenario. LoadGen supports four query-sending scenarios:

1. **Single-Stream**: LoadGen sends a single query to the SUT and waits for response. Upon response, completion time is recorded, and a new query is generated. The metric is 90th percentile latency. This scenario mimics systems where responsiveness is a critical factor such as offline AI queries performed on smartphones.
2. **Multistream**: Queries are sent at a fixed time interval. A Quality of Service constraint is imposed and the metric is the number of streams that the system can process while meeting the QoS constraint. This benchmark reflects systems that process input from multiple sensors.
3. **Server**: LoadGen sends queries according to a Poisson distribution. A benchmark-specific latency bound is defined and only a small number of queries such as 1% for vision can exceed it. The metric is the Poisson parameter representing queries per second that can be processed while meeting the latency bound requirement. This scenario mimics a web service receiving queries from multiple clients.
4. **Offline**: LoadGen sends a single query containing sample data IDs to process. This is the simplest scenario covering batch processing applications and the metric is throughput in samples per second.

LoadGen logs responses during the course of the benchmark and at the end, runs an accuracy script to verify that the responses are valid.

MLPerf Inference has two divisions: closed and open. Most of what has been described above applies to the closed section, which has strict rules to make sure that the results are comparable across different HW and OS toolchains. The open division gives submitters much more freedom, for example, they can change the model or use different metrics. This paper focuses on the closed section.

4 MLPerf Inference Results

So far, one version of vMLPerf Inference benchmark has been released. Numbered 0.5, it was released on November 6th 2019. The following categories were included:

1. Image Classification: ResNet-50 v1.5 with ImageNet data set
2. Image Classification: MobileMet-v1 with ImageNet data set
3. Object Detection: SSD w/ MobileNet-v1 with COCO data set
4. Object Detection: SSD w/ ResNet-34 with COCO 1200 × 1200 data set
5. Translation: NMT with WMT E-G data set.

For each category, all four LoadGen scenarios could be submitted. This results in 20 possible benchmarks.

A total of 37 entries from 13 different vendors were published. None of the entries covered all 20 scenarios, the most was 16 (Nvidia). Most of the submitters were chip-makers: (Nvidia, Intel, Qualcomm, Google, Habana Labs, Alibaba, Centaur Technology, Hailo, FuriosaAI), two from cloud providers (Alibaba, Tencent) and only one from a traditional OEM server vendor (Dell EMC).

Our interest, as a server OEM, is a per-accelerator (or per-CPU) performance comparison. To extract this from MLPerf data, we take Offline scenario results and calculate per-accelerator throughput. The results are shown in Table 1 for 1st, 2nd, and a 3rd placings. Overall, this shows Nvidia's leadership positions with its GPUs taking 9 out of 15 spots and winning 4 of 5 benchmarks. A somewhat surprising result is that of Alibaba's HanGuang 800 inference-only accelerator, which won the ResNet50 Image Classification category by a factor of 4. This accelerator is not well known in and is only available on Alibaba's cloud. Two of the entries belong to a Habana Labs (now part of Intel) accelerator, showing that custom accelerators can provide high performanance and be competive with established chip vendors.

However, this comparison does not include a measure of efficiency. The accelerators being compared have different wattages: for example T4 is rated at 70 W and is being comapred to Xeon 9282 with TDP of 400 W. Currently, computational or power efficiency is not part of MLPerf suite. A work is ongoing on power specification for inference and it is expected to be voluntary once production ready.

Another interesting topic is CPU vs GPU inference performance. We have shown above that GPUs provide better throughput in the offline scenario, but when latency is important, CPUs may provide a better performance. The results in server scenarios - where comparable data between T4 and Xeon 9282 exist – show T4 still being ahead by about the same margin as in the offline scenario. This shows that the PCIe overhead is not very important in a server under load – GPUs (or other acclerators) can batch process incoming data and thus achieve a high efficiency.

Table 1. Best per-accelerator entries in MLPerf Inference v0.5 Offline benchmarks.

	1st place score submitter accelerator	2nd place score submitter accelerator	3rd place score submitter accelerator
Image Recognition MobileNet/ImageNet	17,804 Dell EMC T4	17,474 Alibaba Cloud T4	14,602 Intel Xeon 9282
Image Recognition ResNet/ImageNet	69,307 Alibaba HanGuang 800	16,562 Nvidia Titan RTX	14,451 Habana Synapse
Object Detection SSD/MobileNet COCO	22,945 Nvidia Titan RTX	7609 Nvidia T4	7602 Dell EMC T4
Object Detection SSD/ResNet Coco 1200x1200	415 Nvidia Titan RTX	326 Habana Labs Synapse	164 Google TPU v3
Translation WMT E-G/NMT	1061 Nvidia Titan RTX	771 Google TPUv3	354 Dell EMC T4

5 MLPerf Inference V0.7

MLPerf Inference v0.7 submission deadline is September 2020. The rules for submission and benchmark categories have been modified from the previous version. Importantly, there are two types of submission categories: Data Center and Edge. Benchmarks in each category are different. For Data Center, the following models are available: ResNet, SSD-ResNet, BERT, RNNT, 3D UNET, and DLRM. The edge category replaces DLRM model with SSD-MobileNet. For each benchmark submitters need to submit server and offline scenarios, the only exception being 3D UNET Data Center model where only offline scenario is required. Additional scenarios are not allowed with exception of 3 models in Edge category, where Multi-Stream scenario is allowed.

Overall, this is a step in the right direction. Previous rules, where submitters could pick and choose models and scenarios, resulted cherry-picked submissions, which made fair evaluation of strengths and weaknesses of various accelerators difficult. The new rules will paint a more nuanced picture of AI inference performance.

Our team at Lenovo DCG is preparing to submit to the upcoming Inference v0.7 benchmark. We have partnered with Nvidia and plan to evaluate two GPU-enabled servers: SR670 and SE350. This will cover two different use cases: The first one is a GPU-dense platform for use in the data center, while the latter is an edge device with a single T4 GPU. Our goal is twofold: (i) obtain an officially certified performance scores and (ii) to demonstrate expertise in AI to potential customers.

6 Preliminary Results and Lessons Learned

Our previous work has explored performance evaluation of AI training in a distributed environment [17–20]. We have recently turned our attention to inference with the goal of submitting a score to the upcoming MLPerf Inference v0.7. Our work so far has evaluated performance of various GPUs in an MLPerf-like settings without extensive performance tuning. Our goal has been to compare inference performance of datacenter GPUs rather than to achieve maximum performance. We used docker containers conveniently prepared by Nvidia as a way for others to replicate their posted results. Instructions for executing Inference tests are given in a Nvidia Developer document "Measuring Training and Inferencing Performance on NVIDIA AI Platforms Reviewer's Guide". The document is clear and uses prepared docker containers that include inference-ready models and validation data. The images are publicly available from Nvidia GPU Cloud repository. The downside is that there is no inference server including, thus mimicking the Offline scenario. Additionally, only 1 GPU can be used. Nevertheless, this easy-to-use resource is very useful for quick tests of inference performance.

The results for several types of data center GPUs are given in Table 2. They show that in terms of raw performance, V100S is the highest performing GPU, provides best performance, with T4 taking the last place. To get a measure of power efficiency we estimated performance per Watt by assuming that the cards run at their power ratings. The results are shown in the last row and show that T4, rated at 70 W, provides the best performance per Watt.

Table 2. FP16 Inference Performance of datacenter GPUs. Power efficiency is estimated by dividing measured performance by GPU power ratings.

	V100S	V100 (32 GB)	T4	RTX6000
Performance Images per second	6145	5853	2035	5164
Estimated Performance/watt Images per second per watt	24.6	23.4	29	20.6

While these results provide a lot of insight into inference performance, they are a significant simplification over true MLPerf scores. We are currently in a process of reproducing official MLPerf Inference results from code submitted as a part of the entries. This is still ongoing, and we have met several difficulties when using posted instructions. The process is lengthy as it involves downloading external datasets and installing many dependencies some of which already have newer versions available. Fortunately, MLPerf github repository allows issues to be filed against posted codes and solution to some of the issues can be found there. Even with that, re-using submitted code is time consuming as environment setup and dataset download represent significant hurdles.

With the rapid progress in the AI field, MLPerf serves as both a competition and a benchmark. Our focus as a server OEM is on the latter. Our goal is to have an easy to use toolkit that could be quickly deployed across our server portfolio to gauge and verify their performance. Such a tool would be also useful for server development and design. Additionally, customers increasingly request AI performance data as a part of the purchasing process and thus having MLPerf scores available would make this process easier. However, this is difficult due to the complexity of system setup. A solution to this may be an MLPerf project named MLBox [21] which attempts to package environments and codes into transferable containers. However, this project is still in development and is not ready for production yet.

7 Summary and Conclusions

This paper reviewed current state of AI inference benchmarking. We found that MLPerf Inference is clearly ahead of other efforts having already released a first version of the benchmarks and receiving entries from some of the most important players in the emerging AI industry. This first version shows the value of accelerators across AI inference scenarios, even though compared to CPUs they are subject to PCIe overhead. However, it turns out that accelerators can make up for this by processing incoming requests in large batches, which allows them to utilize their superior processing power.

One of the most valuable aspects of MLPerf has been standardization of AI workloads enabling comparison across the systems. Additionally, the reference implementations and submitter-created codes are free to use, which enables their re-use as either benchmarks or highly tuned performance codes. We have also identified areas for improvements: There is no measure of efficiency or per-device performance and re-use requires significant effort and expertise.

Our own efforts in Inference benchmarking are in progress as we are targeting submission for the MLPerf Inference v0.7. So far, we have greatly benefited from previous submissions and experience gained during the benchmark optimization will be passed on to our Research and Development to guide design of future AI-centric HW platforms.

References

1. He, K., Zhang, X., Ren, S., Sun, J.: Deep residual learning for image recognition. In: Proceedings of the IEEE Conference on Computer Vision and Pattern Recognition, pp. 770–778 (2016)
2. Heber, F., et al.: Sockeye: a toolkit for neural machine translation. arXiv:1712.05690 (2017)
3. Amondei, D., et al.: Deep Speech 2: end-to-end speech recognition in english and mandarin. In: International Conference on Machine Learning, pp. 173–182 (2016)
4. Han, S., Mao, H., Dally, W.J.: Deep compression: Compressing deep neural networks with pruning, trained quantization and Huffman coding. arXiv:1510.00149 (2015)
5. Kanter, D.: Real World Technologies, 25 November 2019. https://www.realworldtech.com/sc19-hpc-meets-machine-learning/
6. Blalock, D., Ortiz, J.J.G., Franle, J., Guttag, J.: What is the state of Neural Network Pruning. In: Proceedings of the 3rd MLSys Conference (2020)
7. Bhandare, A., et al.: Efficient 8-bit quantization of transformer neual machine langage translation model. In: 36th International Conference on Machine Learning (2019)

8. Sung, W., Shin, S., Hwang, K.: Resiliency of deep neural networks under quantization. arXiv: 1511.06488 (2016)
9. Bourrasset, C., et al.: Requirements for an enterprise AI benchmark. In: Nambiar, R., Poess, M. (eds.) TPCTC 2018. LNCS, vol. 11135, pp. 71–81. Springer, Cham (2019). https://doi. org/10.1007/978-3-030-11404-6_6
10. Bench Research: Deep Bench. https://github.com/baidu-research/DeepBench
11. Coleman, C.A., et al.: DAWNBench: an end-to-end deep learning benchmark and competition. In: Proceedings of the 31st Conference on Neural Information Processing Systems (NIPS 2017) (2017)
12. MLPerf. https://www.mlperf.org/
13. Reddy, V.J., et al.: MLPerf Inference Benchmark. arXiv preprint arXiv:1911:02549 (2019)
14. Nambiar, R., Ghandeharizadeh, S., Little, G., Boden, C., Dholakia, A.: Industry panel on defining industry standards for benchmarking artificial intelligence. In: Nambiar, R., Poess, M. (eds.) TPCTC 2018. LNCS, vol. 11135, pp. 1–6. Springer, Cham (2019). https://doi.org/ 10.1007/978-3-030-11404-6_1
15. TPC Press Release: Transaction Processing Performance Council (TPC) Establishes Artificial Intelligence Working Group (TPC-AI) (2017). https://www.businesswire.com/news/home/ 20171212005281/en/Transaction-Processing-Performance-Council-Establishes-Artificial
16. Rabl, T., et al.: ADABench - Towards an industry standard benchmark for advanced analytics. In: Nambiar, R., Poess, M. (eds.) TPCTC 2019. LNCS, vol. 12257, pp. 47–63. Springer, Cham (2020). https://doi.org/10.1007/978-3-030-55024-0_4
17. Hodak, M., Ellison, D., Seidel, P., Dholakia, A.: Performance implications of big data in scalable deep learning: on the importance of bandwidth and caching. In: 2018 IEEE International Conference on Big Data, pp. 1945–1950 (2018). https://doi.org/10.1109/BigData.2018.862 1896
18. Hodak, M., Dholakia, A.: Towards evaluation of tensorflow performance in a distributed compute environment. In: Nambiar, R., Poess, M. (eds.) TPCTC 2018. LNCS, vol. 11135, pp. 82–93. Springer, Cham (2019). https://doi.org/10.1007/978-3-030-11404-6_7
19. Hodak, M., Gorkovenko, M., Dholakia, A.: Towards power efficiency in deep learning on data center hardware. In: 2019 IEEE International Conference on Big Data, pp. 1814–1820 (2019). https://doi.org/10.1109/BigData47090.2019.9005632
20. Hodak, M., Dholakia, A.: Challenges in distributed MLPerf. In: Nambiar, R., Poess, M. (eds.) TPCTC 2019. LNCS, vol. 12257, pp. 39–46. Springer, Cham (2020). https://doi.org/10.1007/ 978-3-030-55024-0_3
21. MLPerf: MLBox. https://github.com/mlperf/mlbox. Accessed 24 July 2020

Analysis of Benchmark Development Times in the Transaction Processing Performance Council and Ideas on How to Reduce It with a Domain Independent Benchmark Evolution Model

Meikel Poess[(✉)]

Oracle Corporation, 500 Oracle Parkway, Redwood Shores, CA 94065, USA
Meikel.Poess@oracle.com

Abstract. The Transaction Processing Performance Council (TPC) has a very successful history of disseminating objective and verifiable performance data to the industry. However, it lacks the ability to create new benchmarks in a timely fashion. In its initial years, the TPC defined benchmarks in about two years on average while recently this number increased to about eight years.

Although TPC benchmarks measure fundamental performance characteristics of transaction systems, which do not change quickly over time, new feature development, e.g. SQL language cannot be ignored.

This paper analyses the reasons for this increased development time and proposes ideas on how to improve benchmark development time by using a domain independent benchmark evolution model.

Keywords: Benchmark development · Databases · Performance analysis

1 Introduction

For over 20 years the Transaction Processing Performance Council (TPC) has been very successful in disseminating objective and verifiable performance data for transaction processing and databases in various domains, i.e. Online Transaction Processing (OLTP), Decision Support (DS) and Web Application (APP). It developed the four OLTP benchmark specification, TPC-A, TPC-B, TPC-C and TPC-E, which to date produced over 1000 benchmark publications. The TPC also developed three decision support benchmark specifications, TPC-D, TPC-H and TPC-R, which produced to date a total of 146 benchmark results and two web benchmark specifications, TPC-W and TPC-App, which produced a total of four results.

In the first years after the TPC was founded it took the TPC about one year to develop a new benchmark specification, now it is taking closer to ten years. TPC's first OLTP benchmark specification, TPC-A, was published in November 1989. Built upon Jim Gray's DebitCredit benchmark TPC-A formalized the rules, which all vendors

© Springer Nature Switzerland AG 2021
R. Nambiar and M. Poess (Eds.): TPCTC 2020, LNCS 12752, pp. 103–111, 2021.
https://doi.org/10.1007/978-3-030-84924-5_8

had to obey in order to publish a benchmark result. About one year later, TPC-B was born. TPC-B was a modification of TPC-A, using the same transaction type (banking transaction), but eliminating the network and user interaction components of the TPC-A workload. The result was a batch transaction processing benchmark. Two years later in June 1992, TPC's third OLTP benchmark specification, TPC-C, was approved after about four years of development. Compared to previous OLTP benchmarks, the TPC-C benchmark is more complex because of its multiple transaction types, more complex database schema and more complex overall execution rules. In the first 15 months after approval TPC-C underwent three major revisions (Version 2 and 3). All three versions were comparable. After a failed Version 4 attempt, in October 2000, Version 5 of TPC-C was approved. This version was non-comparable to previous versions. In 2006 TPC-E, TPC's latest OLTP benchmark was approved after 6 years of development. TPC-E further increases complexity, e.g. TPC-E defines 33 tables, compared to 9 tables in TPC-C.

A similar pattern can be found with TPC's decision support benchmarks. TPC-D, TPC's first decision support benchmark, was approved in May 1995 after four years of development. TPC-D underwent one major backward compatible revision in 1998 before it was replaced by TPC-H and TPC-R in 1999. The replacement benchmarks, TPC-H and TPC-R were based on TPC-D with only some minor execution rules and query changes [2]. Development took about one year of development. Because of lack of market support TPC-R was decommissioned in 1996 because only a couple results were ever published. Since 2000 the TPC has been struggling to publish its next generation decision support benchmark (Table 1). The above data is taken from a historic overview of the TPC by Kim Shanley [1] and general council minutes [4] .

These historic patterns lead to two conclusions: First, while it took about one to two ears for new benchmark developments in the beginning years of the TPC, it takes now about five + years. TPC-C took four years, TPC-E took about six years to develop and TPC-DS, which took 10 years to develop. Second, revising existing benchmark is taking about one to two years. However, the TPC has no strong history of non-comparable revisions of a benchmark. It almost appears as if the TPC, rather than releasing a non-comparable revision of a benchmark, it releases a new benchmark with a new name.

There are good reasons for keeping benchmarks comparable for a long period: It usually takes the engineering teams a year to familiarize themselves with a new benchmark, i.e. develop a benchmark kit, identify the best hardware and software combination to run the benchmark and potentially develop new hardware and design new algorithms. Hardware and software development cycles are usually measured in years, and since hardware and software vendors are interested in showing continues incremental performance increase from release one release cycle to another it is pertinent that comparable versions of a benchmark are around for reasonable time. Furthermore, TPC benchmarks are complex benchmarks often involving vast amount of engineering resources and capital investments. Hence, vendors are interested in using benchmark results as long as possible for marketing purposes.

Contrary, benchmarks can get obsolete if technology advances or applications' needs change. For instance, the structured query language SQL is constantly evolving by adding more complex operators. The SQL 99 standard has added many analytical functions.

Table 1. TPC benchmark history

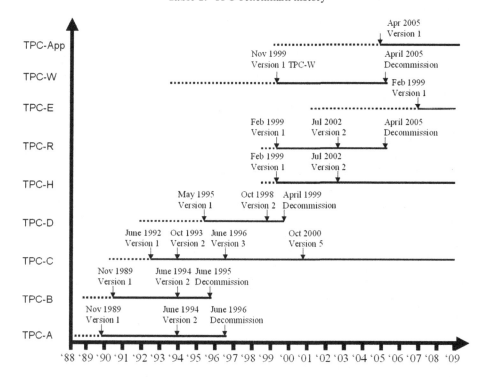

Advances in solid-state drives are changing the way I/O systems are built. Extraction Transformation and Load, which Data warehouse applications are increasingly demanding real time updates from an OLTP system, a.k.a. Trickle Updates.

Although the TPC has very well defined benchmark development processes that cover both new benchmark developments and revisions to existing benchmarks, they are not very effective in allowing for a reasonable continuity of benchmark specifications while, at the same time, in keeping existing benchmarks relevant to the market.

In this paper we present a domain independent benchmark evolution model for the TPC that will give vendors a tool for testing and marketing their systems and software, while also keeping existing benchmarks relevant to the market.

The remainder of this paper is organized as follows. Section 2 gives an overview of TPC's current benchmark development processes, evaluating the strengths and weaknesses of these processes. Section 3 presents the Benchmark Evolution Model and develops wording changes that can be applied directly to the current TPC policies to implement the model. Using a paper exercise Sect. 4 shows how the proposed Benchmark Evolution Model could have kept TPC-H relevant to today's technologies.

2 TPC Background

This section gives an overview of those operational concepts of the TPC that are important in understanding subsequent sections.

The TPC is organized hierarchically. On top of the TPC organization is the General Council (GC). GC makes all decisions during a General Council Meeting in which each member company of the TPC has one vote. A two-thirds vote is required to pass any motion. During these meetings the GC receives feedback from subcommittees in form of subcommittee status reports.

There are standing subcommittees and technical subcommittees. The standing sub-committees are the Steering Committee (SC), the Technical Advisory Board (TAB) and the Public Relations Committee (PRC). Technical subcommittees are permanent com-mittees that supervise and manage administrative, public relations and documentation issues for the TPC. The Steering Committee (SC) consists of five representatives, elected annually, from member companies. The SC is responsible for overseeing TPC adminis-tration and support activities and for providing overall direction and recommendations to the Full Council. Technical Advisory Board (TAB) is tasked with maintaining document and change control over the complex benchmark proposals and methodologies. In addi-tion, the TAB studies issues involving interpretation/compliance of TPC specifications and makes recommendations to the Council. The Public Relations Committee (PRC is tasked with promoting the TPC and establishing the TPC benchmarks as industry standards.

If the GC decides to take on new endeavors, such as developing a new benchmark or defining a term, e.g. processor, it delegates these work items by creating technical subcommittees. Member companies can join and leave subcommittees at any time with approval of the GC.

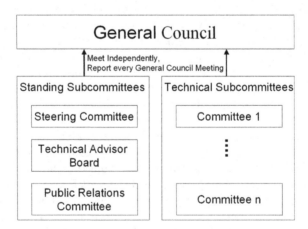

Fig. 1. Hierarchical structure of the TPC.

All major decisions, the TPC takes, especially those that affect benchmark specifications, require a super majority to pass. Only procedural decisions, such as voting on committee members require a simple majority. A super majority is defined as two-thirds of the member companies present and voting, excluding abstentions. A simple majority is defined as greater than 50% of member companies present and voting. The super majority rule guarantees strong consensus on important issues among member companies.

3   TPC's Current Benchmark Development Processes

The TPC has two means to develop benchmark specifications. New benchmark specifications are developed following the *Benchmark Development Cycle* as defined in Sect. 3.1 of the TPC policies [3]. Revisions of existing benchmark specifications are developed following the *Revisions to a TPC Benchmark Standard* as defined in Sect. 3.2 of the TPC policies [3]. In this section we will briefly review these two processes and discuss their advantages and disadvantages so that the reader has a better understanding of the Benchmark Evolution Model proposed in Sect. 4.

3.1   Benchmark Development Cycle

New benchmark development must follow the nine-step development process, which is outlined in Fig. 2 below. Each box symbolizes one of the nine steps of the development process. The shaded boxes indicate that the general council needs to take action, usually by voting on a motion, the others involve extensive development and testing efforts of technical subcommittee members.

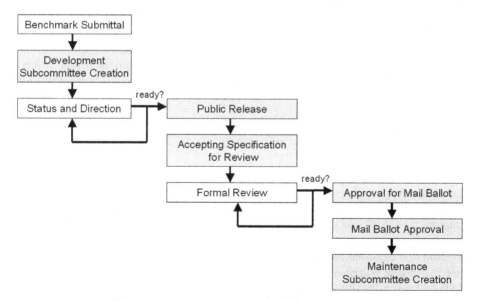

Fig. 2. TPC's current benchmark development cycle.

Benchmark Submittal
Member companies submit an idea for a standard specification in a format similar to TPC Benchmark Standards. If the General Council accepts the proposal a development subcommittee is created to develop the final specification. Depending on the resources that are spent to develop the benchmark idea into a benchmark specification this step can take anywhere between 6 months to 2 years.

Creation of a Subcommittee
This is a formal step taken by the General Council to establish and empower a development subcommittee to develop a formal benchmark specification.

Status and Direction
This step is an iterative process. At each General Meeting, which is held approximately every 2 months, the development subcommittee provides a status update on its work, including a working draft of the Specification. During this meeting the Council provides direction and feedback to the subcommittee to further their work.

Authorizing Public Release of Draft Specification
Once the General Council is convinced that the specification is almost ready it authorizes the release of a draft Specification to the public. Releasing a specification to the public encourages companies to implement the draft specification, to gather more experimental data, and to speed-up the approval of a specification.

Accepting a Standard for Review
When the subcommittee feels that the Specification is of sufficient quality to be considered for formal review and approval, it submits the Specification to the Council for approval to advance into formal review.

Formal Review
In this phase, the specification is made available to all TPC members and the public for formal review. All comments and proposed changes generated from the review will be posted in the comment database and considered by the development subcommittee for resolution. This step can take 6 months to 3 years.

Approval for Mail Ballot
This is a formal step the General Council takes to approve the updated benchmark specification for mail ballot.

Mail Ballot Approval
This is a formal ballot to approve the benchmark specification as a standard. Each member company can submit one vote to either approve, disapprove or abstain the ballot.

Creation of a Maintenance Subcommittee
If the mail ballot is approved general council establishes a maintenance subcommittee, which will automatically supersede the development subcommittee.

3.2 Revisions to an Existing Benchmark Specification Standard

The version number of a TPC benchmark specification comprises of three tiers. A revision to an existing benchmark specification can either be a third tier, minor or major revision. Unless the general council stipulates otherwise revisions of the same benchmark specification are comparable. However, in practice this is only true for third tier and minor revisions. In general major revisions are non-comparable since they alter the benchmark workload.

Third tier changes clarify confusing or ambiguous areas of the benchmark specification. They do not alter the workload or specification's intent or meaning. Minor revisions entail changes that may alter the workload, intent, or meaning of the benchmark specification. However, the changes are such that benchmark publications that are published under new revision are still comparable to the prior version. Major revision changes alter the workload so significantly or alter the intent of the benchmark specification so drastically such that benchmark publications following the new version are incomparable with older versions.

4 Benchmark Evolution Model

As explained in Sect. 3 the TPC has very well-defined benchmark development processes that cover both new benchmark developments and revisions to existing benchmarks. They have created a handful of powerful benchmarks in the beginning years of the TPC. However, as we will explain in the first part of this section, in the second decade of the TPC it turns out they are not very effective in creating new benchmarks and they are not very successful in allowing for a reasonable continuity of benchmark specifications while, at the same time, in keeping existing benchmarks relevant to the market. In the second part of this section we will explain a new benchmark development process that is more effective in generating new benchmark specifications while still preserving benchmark specification continuity.

4.1 Weaknesses of TPC's Existing Benchmark Development Processes

TPC's development cycle for new benchmarks is too long. As the analysis in Sect. 1 has shown the time to develop and accept new benchmarks within the TPC is on average between four to six years. Considering that technology changes every one to two years and application usage of transactional systems follow market demands, which usually changes at a rate faster then four to six years, benchmarks that take more than two years to develop miss their market relevance.

There are multiple reasons for TPC's long benchmark development cycle. Member companies joining development subcommittees in the middle of its development cycle distract the development process and may lead to an extended development time because they bring in their own requirements, which may change the development direction. When a development subcommittee is created (see second step in Fig. 2) interested member companies are asked to join. It is not uncommon that only a subset of the TPC membership joins a given subcommittee, because not every member company has a vested interest in a particular new benchmark. It is also common that interested member companies do not have the resources to actively contribute to a benchmark development. Active contribution to the development of a benchmark means to design concepts, write code or test code. Changes in member companies' business agendas or funding may then trigger to join a particular development subcommittee. Lastly, new member companies may join subcommittees upon joining the TPC.

New benchmark developments usually require new benchmark tools, such as workload generators, workload drivers, auditing and result documentation tools. Developing these tools is very time consuming and resource intensive, because they are "one of its kind" tools, suited to specific benchmarks. Furthermore, they have to perform and work on all member companies' platforms. In order to assess the complexity of data and query generators please refer to [5,6].

To summarize, here are the reasons for long benchmark development:

1) Lack of adequate time and resource commitment from TPC companies.
2) Different people joining the development subcommittee at different times. As a result decisions are being overhauled frequently.
3) New benchmark development requires complex tools.
4) New benchmark requires extensive testing from vendors.
5) Companies can join an existing effort at any time, which in many cases is a distraction and not a boost to the benchmark development.
6) Companies who do not participate in a benchmark development effort can vote against benchmark.

4.2 Overcoming the Shortages of TPC's Development Model

One of the most progressive steps so far the TPC has taken to shorten its long benchmark development cycles was to allow express benchmarks. Express benchmarks have reduced the development time significantly by leveraging existing tools and workloads. For instance, TPCx-BB leveraged the workload of TPC-DS. It amended a subset of TPC-DS with more workloads. TPCx-IoT is based on ???. By taking existing benchmarks/workloads and kits the TPC was able to develop these express benchmarks in a couple of years. In addition, these benchmarks provide a Tool Kit that allows for anybody with very little knowledge of the benchmark to run them.

The drawback of Kit based benchmarks is that they cannot be easily adapted to new technology. A specification-based benchmark, i.e. Enterprise Benchmarks, allow for emerging technologies to be used.

The key takeaway from express benchmarks is the reuse of existing tools and workloads. The TPC already has a very large repository of workloads and tools. In order to leverage these workloads and tools, the TPC must provide ways to evolve these benchmarks into new benchmarks. This will enable benchmark developers to not only reuse existing workloads and tools, but also allow for benchmark to evolve naturally. For instance, TPC-H contains 22 queries, which took a long time to develop, test agree upon by subcommittee members. If the TPC allowed for benchmark to evolve, TPC-H could have been released with 10 queries and later amended with another 10 queries. If the TPC gets this right, there could be a larger or modified set of queries every couple of years. Of course, this would stress the reporting of benchmark results as multiple version of the same benchmark would be available at any given time. The TPC would need to develop rules for "aging" of benchmark versions and for allowing results to be present from different versions.

The second most important change the TPC must implement to reduce benchmark development time is to disallow every member company regardless whether they participated in the development of a benchmark or not to decide whether the benchmark becomes an official TPC benchmark or not. Only those companies who had participated in the development of the benchmark should be allowed to vote. I would go even so far as to disallow companies to join a subcommittee after it started developing a benchmark.

References

1. Shanley, K.: Chief Operating Officer, Transaction Processing Performance Council: "History and Overview of the TPC". http://www.tpc.org/information/about/history.asp
2. Poess, M., Floyd, C.: New TPC benchmarks for decision support and web commerce. ACM SIGMOD RECORD **29**(4), 64–71 (2000)
3. Transaction Processing Performance Council Policies Version 5.17.http://www.tpc.org/inform ation/about/documentation/spec/TPC_Policies_v5.17.pdf
4. TPC General Council Minutes. http://www.tpc.org/Members_Only/GenMtgMinutes/GenMtg Min.html
5. Stephens, J.M., Poess, M.: "MUDD: a multi-dimensional data generator". In: WOSP, pp. 104–109 (2004)
6. Poess, M., Stephens, J.M.: Generating thousand benchmark queries in seconds". In: VLDB, pp. 1045–1053 (2004)

Author Index

Printed in the United States
by Baker & Taylor Publisher Services